Endangered Species

Other Books of Related Interest

OPPOSING VIEWPOINTS®

Endangered Species

Helen Cothran, *Book Editor*

David L. Bender, *Publisher*
Bruno Leone, *Executive Editor*
Bonnie Szumski, *Editorial Director*
Stuart B. Miller, *Managing Editor*

OPPOSING
VIEWPOINTS®
SERIES

Greenhaven Press, Inc., San Diego, California

Cover photos:
Elephants: U.S. Fish and Wildlife Service/Miriam Westervest
Manatee: U.S. Fish and Wildlife Service/Galen Rathbun
Peregrine: U.S. Fish and Wildlife Service/Craig Koppie
Gorilla and leopard: John Foxx Images

Library of Congress Cataloging-in-Publication Data

Endangered species : opposing viewpoints / Helen Cothran, book
editor.
    p.   cm. — (Opposing viewpoints series)
    Includes bibliographical references and index.
    ISBN 0-7377-0505-1 (pbk. : alk. paper) —
ISBN 0-7377-0506-X (lib : alk. paper)
    1. Endangered species. I. Cothran, Helen. II. Opposing
viewpoints series (Unnumbered)

QH75 .E66 2001
333.95'22—dc21   99-085752
                                                    CIP

Greenhaven Press, Inc., P.O. Box 289009
San Diego, CA 92198-9009

"Congress shall make no law...abridging the freedom of speech, or of the press."

First Amendment to the U.S. Constitution

The basic foundation of our democracy is the First Amendment guarantee of freedom of expression. The Opposing Viewpoints Series is dedicated to the concept of this basic freedom and the idea that it is more important to practice it than to enshrine it.

Contents

Why Consider
Opposing Viewpoints?

*"The only way in which a human being can make some
approach to knowing the whole of a subject is by hearing
what can be said about it by persons of every variety of
opinion and studying all modes in which it can be looked
at by every character of mind. No wise man ever acquired
his wisdom in any mode but this."*

John Stuart Mill

In our media-intensive culture it is not difficult to find differing opinions. Thousands of newspapers and magazines
and dozens of radio and television talk shows resound with
differing points of view. The difficulty lies in deciding
which opinion to agree with and which "experts" seem the
most credible. The more inundated we become with differing opinions and claims, the more essential it is to hone
critical reading and thinking skills to evaluate these ideas.
Opposing Viewpoints books address this problem directly
by presenting stimulating debates that can be used to enhance and teach these skills. The varied opinions contained
in each book examine many different aspects of a single issue. While examining these conveniently edited opposing
views, readers can develop critical thinking skills such as the
ability to compare and contrast authors' credibility, facts,
argumentation styles, use of persuasive techniques, and
other stylistic tools. In short, the Opposing Viewpoints Series is an ideal way to attain the higher-level thinking and
reading skills so essential in a culture of diverse and contra-
dictory opinions.

In addition to providing a tool for critical thinking, Opposing Viewpoints books challenge readers to question
their own strongly held opinions and assumptions. Most
people form their opinions on the basis of upbringing,
peer pressure, and personal, cultural, or professional bias.
By reading carefully balanced opposing views, readers
must directly confront new ideas as well as the opinions of

those with whom they disagree. This is not to simplistically argue that everyone who reads opposing views will—or should—change his or her opinion. Instead, the series enhances readers' understanding of their own views by encouraging confrontation with opposing ideas. Careful examination of others' views can lead to the readers' understanding of the logical inconsistencies in their own opinions, perspective on why they hold an opinion, and the consideration of the possibility that their opinion requires further evaluation.

Evaluating Other Opinions

To ensure that this type of examination occurs, Opposing Viewpoints books present all types of opinions. Prominent spokespeople on different sides of each issue as well as well-known professionals from many disciplines challenge the reader. An additional goal of the series is to provide a forum for other, less known, or even unpopular viewpoints. The opinion of an ordinary person who has had to make the decision to cut off life support from a terminally ill relative, for example, may be just as valuable and provide just as much insight as a medical ethicist's professional opinion. The editors have two additional purposes in including these less known views. One, the editors encourage readers to respect others' opinions—even when not enhanced by professional credibility. It is only by reading or listening to and objectively evaluating others' ideas that one can determine whether they are worthy of consideration. Two, the inclusion of such viewpoints encourages the important critical thinking skill of objectively evaluating an author's credentials and bias. This evaluation will illuminate an author's reasons for taking a particular stance on an issue and will aid in readers' evaluation of the author's ideas.

As series editors of the Opposing Viewpoints Series, it is our hope that these books will give readers a deeper understanding of the issues debated and an appreciation of the complexity of even seemingly simple issues when good and honest people disagree. This awareness is particularly important in a democratic society such as ours in which people enter into public debate to determine the common good.

Those with whom one disagrees should not be regarded as enemies but rather as people whose views deserve careful examination and may shed light on one's own.

Thomas Jefferson once said that "difference of opinion leads to inquiry, and inquiry to truth." Jefferson, a broadly educated man, argued that "if a nation expects to be ignorant and free . . . it expects what never was and never will be." As individuals and as a nation, it is imperative that we consider the opinions of others and examine them with skill and discernment. The Opposing Viewpoints Series is intended to help readers achieve this goal.

David L. Bender & Bruno Leone,
Series Editors

Greenhaven Press anthologies primarily consist of previously published material taken from a variety of sources, including periodicals, books, scholarly journals, newspapers, government documents, and position papers from private and public organizations. These original sources are often edited for length and to ensure their accessibility for a young adult audience. The anthology editors also change the original titles of these works in order to clearly present the main thesis of each viewpoint and to explicitly indicate the opinion presented in the viewpoint. These alterations are made in consideration of both the reading and comprehension levels of a young adult audience. Every effort is made to ensure that Greenhaven Press accurately reflects the original intent of the authors included in this anthology.

Introduction

"As Congress continues to mull over sweeping changes in the Endangered Species Act and the Wise Use movement continues to fight reintroduction, the future of federal intervention on behalf of rare plants and animals may be determined by the direction the condor takes."
—*Todd Wilkinson*, National Parks, *May/June 1996.*

An eighty-three-year-old man living in a remote mountain town in California heard strange noises upstairs in his bedroom and climbed the stairs to investigate. What he saw amazed him: Eight huge black birds had torn through the screen door and were wreaking havoc in his bedroom. Les Reid, the man whose home was broken into, said of his discovery, "I wasn't mad, I was just astonished."

The birds that Reid found in his home in 1999 were California condors, part of a flock of 29 birds that were bred in captivity and then reintroduced into their native habitat in the Los Padres National Forest in 1992 by the U.S. Fish and Wildlife Service (USFWS). Condors—which can live to be 80 years old—have existed in the southwest for 12,000 years, but habitat destruction, hunting, and DDT and lead poisoning depleted the condor population until there were only 27 left in 1987. In 1999, there are 162 birds alive, 113 in captivity, 29 free in California, and 20 more free in Arizona. Efforts to save endangered species like the condor attempt to stem the tide of extinctions that some scientists believe are occurring at an unprecedented rate in Earth's history. The Global Biodiversity Assessment estimates that extinction threatens more than 31,000 plant and animal species today. Although scientists argue about the rate of extinction and its cause, most agree that the price of each extinction is a net loss of biodiversity, the rich variety of species that comprise the food chains which all species—including humans—depend on for survival.

Not all people agree on how to protect species in danger of extinction. Captive breeding and reintroduction programs like the one that rescued the condor represent one side of the debate. Proponents of these programs maintain that habitat destruction necessitates breeding animals in zoos. Charles Hirshberg, writer for *Life* magazine, contends that zoos have "saved threatened animals . . . from extinction." Proponents also maintain that reintroduction—when possible—helps restore the food chains that sustain all life. As Roger Schlickeisen, president of Defenders of Wildlife, claims, "every living thing has some ecological role to play," and, since vultures like the condor eat carrion, they eliminate waste and prevent disease. Those who support captive breeding of the condor maintain that their numbers were dwindling so fast—there were only nine individuals left in 1985—that if they weren't captured and bred, they would go extinct. Thanks to captive breeding programs at the Los Angeles Zoo and the San Diego Wild Animal Park, the status of the condor has been changed by the USFWS from endangered to threatened.

Proponents of captive breeding and reintroduction programs support government regulations like the Endangered Species Act (ESA) of 1973 because, they claim, the ESA has saved many species like the California condor from extinction. They contend that federal restrictions are the only way to mitigate what Garrett Hardin, professor at the University of California at Santa Barbara, calls "the tragedy of the commons." He maintains that "each man is locked into a system that compels him to increase his herd without limit—in a world that is limited." Proponents argue that without the pressure of the ESA and other environmental restrictions, the private actions that have helped save endangered species would never have occurred because landowners—dedicated to their own self-interest—would have had no incentive to protect plants and animals at risk. But, under the threat of increased restrictions on land use, landowners have entered into voluntary agreements that protect the habitats of endangered species.

Opponents of captive breeding and reintroduction programs often make very different arguments in support of their opposition. On the one hand are people who also support government regulation as the best way to protect species, but who argue that the condor program drains money—more than 25 million dollars—away from more important efforts to save the birds. Opponents' largest concern is that breeding and release efforts are a way of avoiding the more complex and pressing problem of preserving the condors' native range which extends across most of North America. They also maintain that most reintroduced animals do not survive in the wild—60 percent of released condors have died, according to one study—and are more susceptible to disease because they lack genetic variability. In addition, opponents are concerned about the condors' fitness for survival in the wild after captivity. They point to the destruction in Les Reid's bedroom as evidence that reintroduced animals are too tame to avoid human contact and will therefore not survive on their own. Fiona Sunquist, a frequent contributor to *International Wildlife*, contends that real ecosystems have proven to be "not at all easy to restock even with a species [they] once held."

Others oppose the condor breeding and release programs on very different grounds. While they too protest the cost, they maintain that the real cost of captive breeding and reintroduction programs is to private landowners. They claim that if endangered species such as reintroduced condors are found on their land, the government will restrict the use of that land under the Endangered Species Act. Such restrictions of land uses such as ranching and mining, they argue, cost private landowners money which the federal government does not reimburse. Robert J. Smith, scholar at the Competitive Enterprise Institute, maintains that this "uncompensated taking of private property" is against the Constitution and threaten landowners' civil rights. Opponents also maintain that such restrictions have had the unintended consequence of encouraging landowners to destroy prime habitat of endangered species in efforts to avoid the costly restrictions, actions that further harm endangered animals. They contend that private initiative would be more effective at saving species than would regulation.

The California condor is a symbol of the plight of endangered species everywhere, and the condor captive breeding and reintroduction program is the battleground on which people fight over how to save animals at risk. While Les Reid may not have been upset that the birds broke into his home, other residents of Pine Mountain Club are perhaps less forgiving. Nearly half of the twenty-nine birds released in the area are now making frequent trips to the town and have made themselves at home there, resting on lodge railings and ripping up deck furniture. Biologists are particularly concerned because such boldness around humans indicates a lack of healthy mistrust of people, an intrepidness found in many reintroduced animals that threatens their ability to survive on their own.

The decision about whether to use captive breeding and reintroduction programs to protect endangered and threatened animals like the condor is an important point of contention in the debate about endangered species. In *Endangered Species: Opposing Viewpoints*, the authors examine extinction and the efforts to prevent it in the following chapters: Is Extinction a Serious Problem? Are Efforts to Preserve Endangered Species Effective? Should Endangered Species Take Priority over Jobs, Development, and Property Rights? How Can Endangered Species Be Protected in Other Countries? In these chapters, the authors debate the responsibility humans have in preserving endangered species.

CHAPTER 1

Is Extinction a Serious Problem?

Chapter Preface

High in the Sierra Nevada, divers searched a clear blue lake for rainbow trout. When they found a fish, they killed it. The divers did not use fishing poles and did not eat the fish—they were state fisheries biologists who had killed over three thousand trout one summer to help save a native amphibian, the mountain yellow-legged frog—whose tadpoles are the trout's favorite food—from extinction.

The rainbow trout found in that lake and in virtually all freshwater lakes and streams in the Sierra were planted there over the years by the State of California for the enjoyment of recreational anglers. However, many biologists maintain that the introduction of non-native species—exotics—which scientists call "bioinvasion," threatens biological diversity. Don C. Schmitz claims that "exotic species have contributed to the decline of 42 percent of U.S. endangered and threatened species." E.O. Wilson adds, "extinction by the invasion of exotic species is like death by disease: gradual, insidious, requiring scientific methods to diagnose." Non-native species can wipe out entire populations of native species, diminishing the biodiversity vital to environmental and human health.

Not everyone agrees that bioinvasion is a problem, however. When biologists began killing the trout in the Sierra lakes, for example, a local said, "it's cutting into the public's use and enjoyment of these lakes." Other commentators claim that the U.S. government wastes millions of dollars on programs to eradicate non-native species introduced initially by the government itself. Some critics like Robert A. Condry claim that if extinction of native species does occur, it is a natural phenomenon and point to the dinosaurs as proof. Extinction, they say, can be beneficial by culling out weaker species and improving the health of ecosystems. Finally, deciding what is "native" and what is "exotic" is fruitless, critics argue, because species constantly move around geographically.

Oblivious to the debate surrounding it, the mountain yellow-legged frog enjoys protection from trout, at least for now. But questions about endangered species persist. The authors in the following chapter explore whether or not extinction is a serious problem.

> "*Without regard, [we] continue to remove species from delicate ecosystems—a course that could lead to total collapse of those systems.*"

Extinction Is a Serious Problem

Edward J. Maruska

Although extinction of plant and animal species has always occurred, many scientists today believe that human activity has accelerated extinction rates. In the following viewpoint, Edward J. Maruska, executive director of the Cincinnati Zoo and Botanical Garden, estimates that one hundred plant and animal species may be lost per day. Maruska argues that phenomenal human population growth causes the destruction of habitats and the overhunting that leads to extinction. When one species becomes extinct, he contends, other species follow, creating a "domino effect" which can destroy the natural balance on which humans depend for survival.

As you read, consider the following questions:

1. According to Maruska, how many animal species were lost each day from 1990 to 1995?
2. Why, according to Maruska, are island species more vulnerable to extinction?
3. How much of the world's rain forest has the Earth lost, according to the author?

Excerpted from "The Pace of Extinction," by Edward Maruska. This article appeared in the May 1999 issue and is reprinted with permission from *The World & I*, a publication of The Washington Times Corporation, copyright ©1999.

Even as early man began to colonize his world, he set in motion the catalysts that would lead to the extinction of many wild species. Islands became the first to suffer from the ill effects of man's colonization and the introduction of animals alien to those habitats. Wherever early island colonization took place, extinction occurred. The large, flightless moa birds of New Zealand were hunted by the early Maori and extirpated in short order once colonization began. The island continent of Australia, which may have been colonized 30,000–50,000 years ago, saw the extinction of almost all its large marsupial and reptile species—including the giant wombat, giant kangaroo, and great monitor lizard.

Islands and Continents at Risk

Madagascar, isolated from Africa at an early stage, became almost a living laboratory of evolution. Man's presence, however, proved a continual threat to that unique world reserve, leading to the extinction of many species, including the giant lemur, Madagascan hippopotamus, and elephant bird. Today, mainly because of man's overpopulation of the island and indiscriminate use of resources, all lemurs are threatened, as are many other mammals, amphibians, reptiles, birds, and plants.

A similar scenario occurred during the colonization of major landmasses. In the Northern Hemisphere, for example, early man may have played a significant role in the extinction of a number of megavertebrates—such as the mammoths, mastodons, giant sloths, and woolly rhinoceros—as well as their predators, including the saber-toothed cat and the dire wolf.

From the time of Christ until the year 1800, man contributed to the loss of one animal species every 55 years or so. From 1800 to 1900, the rate was one species every year and a half, and from 1900 to 1990, that rate accelerated to one animal species per year. From 1990 to 1995, at least three forms of animal life were lost each day. In his recent book *Life in the Balance: Humanity and the Biodiversity Crisis*, Niles Eldredge states that we are now losing approximately 30,000 plant and animal species a year. This figure (which includes numerous low-profile insects and microbes essential to a healthy ecosystem) amounts to a staggering 82.2 species a day! With the continuing destruction of rain forests, it seems quite likely we could lose 100 plant and animal species a day as we approach the next millennium.

The Last of Its Kind

On September 1, 1914, there was a huddle of personnel around a solitary cage at the Cincinnati Zoo. Everyone, including the zoo director, was staring at the last of what was once among the most abundant of land vertebrate species. Martha, the last passenger pigeon, had died.

During the early nineteenth century, ornithologists John Audubon and Alexander Wilson recorded that when the passenger pigeon migrated from its winter feeding grounds to nesting locations, the flock would be miles wide and last for days. The birds would darken the sky, and their wingbeats would drown out all sound nearby. Around 1850, their numbers were estimated to be as many as nine billion. But the passenger pigeon was hunted indiscriminately for food and target practice and slaughtered by the millions. By 1871–1880, the bird was rendered "biologically" extinct—that is, its population was so severely reduced that normal breeding patterns were compromised. The last survivor in the wild was seen in 1900 in Sargents, Ohio.

Then in 1918, Incas—the only surviving Carolina parakeet—died at the Cincinnati Zoo. It represented the single parrot species that nested in the United States. While primarily a southern species, it had been reported as far north as New York. The parakeet had been hunted down as an agricultural pest, because it would descend on orchards and destroy the fruit. The millinery industry and the popularity of feathered hats also played a role in its extinction and in the near extinction of various other North American birds, including the American egret.

The Cincinnati Zoo had the unfortunate distinction of overseeing the demise of two once-abundant species. Our zoo staff has vowed never to let that happen again, and we are working hard to save species, no matter how difficult. We are now known worldwide for our successes in breeding endangered species.

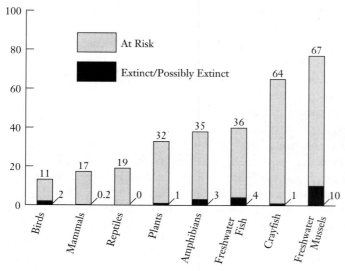

Species Extinct and at Risk in North America (percentage by group)

Note: Top numbers include both "at risk" and "extinct." Bottom numbers refer to "extinct" only.

Source: The Nature Conservancy and the Network of Natural Heritage Programs and Conservation Data Centres, 1995.

Thankfully, the American bison was saved from a similar fate. With the development of the West, 50 million bison disappeared from the plains. Had it not been for private reserves and the New York Zoological Society, the National Zoo, and the Cincinnati Zoo, the species might not have survived. We would have lost a part of our heritage.

Species in Trouble

In the United States, the Endangered Species Act of 1973 has led to the identification of species that are endangered or threatened. An "endangered" species can be defined as a species that is in danger of extinction throughout all or a significant portion of its range. A "threatened" species is likely to become endangered within the foreseeable future, in all or a significant portion of its range.

Because of the rapidity of change in the wild and the paucity of survey work in the world's remote areas, it is difficult to give an exact accounting of the number of species considered endangered or threatened on a global scale. In the *1996 IUCN Red List of Threatened Animals*, the World Conservation Union stated that 5,205 animal species were either critically endangered or vulnerable to extinction. This number represented an increase of about 1,000 since the 1990 list. On a national level, recent figures from the U.S. Fish and Wildlife Service (USFWS) indicate that 924 native species of plants and animals are endangered and 255 are threatened. The agency has 518 approved recovery plans.

I think that the real dilemma is the phenomenal increase in our own numbers, leading to the overuse of resources. When I entered the zoo profession as a young man, the global human population was about 2 billion. Population biologists were predicting that by the time I reached retirement age, which I am approaching, that number would be 5 billion. Today it is nearing 6 billion. It is estimated that by the year 2030, there may be 10 billion people straining the capabilities of our planet.

Population Pressures on Wildlife

The pressures on wildlife will continue to increase as long as our burgeoning population creates more waste and pollutes the land, water, and air. More natural resources will be used, as more forests are cut down, more wetlands are drained, and more land is plowed or converted into shopping and industrial centers. Moreover, by continuing to introduce animal and plant species into innumerable nonnative habitats, we often pave the way for wreaking havoc on native species.

As in the beginning, island species are likely to be the first to suffer from these numerous pressures. Islands have a more delicate balance of fauna and flora, and they have seen more extinctions than the vast landmasses. Areas that are currently struggling with the loss of species include the islands of Hawaii, Borneo, and Sumatra. If we do not resolve our population expansion, islands may prove to be microcosms of what could happen on the larger landmasses in the future.

For instance, the Sumatran rhinoceros, one of the rarest of five rhino species, may number only 200 in the wild. To determine if they could be bred in captivity, some of these animals were salvaged from areas that were about to be logged out. The Cincinnati Zoo is home to three of them. So far, we have had three unsuccessful pregnancies, but we have learned a great deal and hope to unlock the secrets of their reproductive behavior.

Extinctions Cause Destruction of Vital Ecosystems

The current extinction rate of species ranges from approximately 1000 to 10,000 times higher than natural extinction rates, and if this trend continues, as many as 2 million species of plants and animals will be exterminated worldwide by the middle of the next century. This forecast is alarming because biodiversity is essential for the sustainable functioning of the agricultural, forest, and natural ecosystems on which humans depend. For example, the loss of a key species (e.g., a pollinator) can cause the collapse of an ecosystem.

David Pimentel, *BioScience*, December 1997.

Other ecosystems—such as the rain forests of South America, Asia, and Africa—continue to see tremendous pressures on their natural resources. At one time, 25 percent of the world's land surface was clothed in rain forests. Today that figure has dwindled to 6 percent, yet the pressure for resources from these areas continues. Ironically, half the world's remaining diversity of species is contained in that 6 percent. It is therefore critical that we stem the loss of these habitats. Not only are we losing plants and animals faster than their benefits can be studied, we are also creating problems for the indigenous human populations that live off the land.

The Importance of Extinction

Stanford University biologist Paul Ehrlich was once asked why all these species are important. His succinct answer was that if you knew someone had removed a rivet or two from an airplane you were in, it wouldn't really bother you. But if he kept removing rivets, you would be very hesitant about stepping into that aircraft. Yet we, without regard, continue to remove species from delicate ecosystems—a course that could lead to total collapse of those systems.

Aldo Leopold, regarded as the father of modern wildlife management, said it best when he referred to the smaller species of animals and plants as the "small parts" of an ecosystem. In his view, they are just as important as the larger species, because when you start to weed out species from any ecosystem, you upset the natural balance formed over millions of years and initiate a domino effect all down the line. As Leopold cautioned, "To keep every cog and wheel is the first precaution of intelligent tinkering."

Habitat preservation is paramount. But since man has "tinkered" with the wild world, and not always intelligently, I think we have an obligation to save as many species as we can, even if it means breeding them in captivity. As the state of the art in wildlife management improves, it will become increasingly feasible to foster certain wild populations by reintroducing species bred in captivity. Zoos and wildlife departments around the world have consolidated their efforts to work with a small number of species that lend themselves to these efforts.

> *"The 'rediscovery' of sundry species long believed to be extinct has become . . . commonplace."*

Extinction Is Not a Serious Problem

Robert W. Lee

In the following viewpoint, Robert W. Lee argues that scientists overstate the extinction problem by labeling species extinct when people no longer observe living specimens. However, the frequent rediscovery of living organisms previously labeled extinct, he claims, indicates that a classification system based solely on personal observation cannot adequately measure extinction rates. Furthermore, Lee asserts, when extinction does occur, it most likely improves the environment rather than harms it. Lee is a frequent contributor to *New American*, a conservative magazine.

As you read, consider the following questions:

1. According to Lee, how many coelacanths do "hand-wringers" now estimate exist?
2. What, according to the author, happened to the pair of newly discovered Edwards' Pheasants once captured?
3. How was the pygmy blue-tongue lizard rediscovered, according to Lee?

Reprinted, with permission, from "Return of the 'Extincts,'" by Robert W. Lee, *The New American*, February 16, 1998.

The "rediscovery" of sundry species long believed to be extinct has become so commonplace that it has been proposed that such animals and plants be collectively reclassified as a new species, *Marktwainus remindsus*, since the reports of their demise were so egregiously exaggerated.

We are constantly being told, it seems, by gravely concerned global environmentalists, that our planet is losing plant and animal species at a rate of 50, or 100, or 150, or more, each and every day. Harvard University biologist E.O. Wilson, a leading guru of global environmentalism, has claimed that nearly 140 species are being destroyed daily in rain forests alone.

Measuring Extinction Rates

Such guesstimates vary widely because they lack credible, verifiable evidence. No one has ever actually witnessed the demise of even a single species. Indeed, the standard for "extinction" is simply man's inability to find specimens of a given species over a given period of time. In January 1996, for instance, it was claimed that the last living Polynesian tree snail had breathed its last at the London Zoo. One news account reported that the tiny mollusk's tombstone would include the inscription: "1.5 million years BC to January 1996." Yet for all we know, the snails may still exist somewhere, and simply be slow in reaching a point where humans notice them (they travel two feet per year, tops).

The alleged demise of the Polynesian tree snail was depicted as an environmental tragedy. Yet the extinction of some species, which are superseded by others, is an entirely natural phenomenon. Only in an age of unprecedented government meddling and coercion under the guise of "protecting the environment" could the preservation of every creature known to man become a fashionable political mantra. The knee-jerk assumption that the disappearance of this or that dwindling species would harm the planet is questionable. The odds are about even that it would actually enhance the environment by, for example, making way for more advanced species of far greater value.

The coelacanth, which is now oxymoronically characterized as a "living fossil" by scientists anxious to mitigate their mistake in stamping it extinct, is a large, blue fish with white spots and leg-like fins that was assumed to have disappeared with the dinosaurs 70 million, 80 million, or as many as 400 million years ago (depending on the source). But in December 1938 a fisherman netted one off the coast of South Africa. In December 1952 another was caught near the Comorian island of Anjouan. In 1991, one was trawled near Maputo, Mozambique. And yet another was netted off Madagascar in 1995.

Today, the total catch of this fascinating (if somewhat physically repulsive) fish probably exceeds 200, most of which have been hauled up from the deep waters off Anjouan and Grand Camore islands. Some hand-wringers now estimate that there may be no more than 500 still in existence, but that figure, reminiscent of the wrong-headed claim that the fish had become extinct, is mere speculation based on limited surveys of incomplete coelacanth populations. For instance, it is not known if the Comorian colony is the only one. Specimens caught elsewhere could be strays from the Comoros, but on the other hand they could be from undiscovered free-standing colonies in areas where fishing practices are not conducive to catching coelacanths. Again, for all we know there may be tens of thousands lurking in and about deep-water caves worldwide, rather than the relative handful now claimed by scientists who once thought there were none at all.

Some Misclassifications

Following are a few other notable instances of premature extinction:

• *Woolly Flying Squirrel.* In June 1995 it was reported that a woolly flying squirrel, presumed extinct for 70 years, had reappeared among the Himalayan clifftops of Pakistan. The rediscovery startled Dr. Charles Woods, a member of the Florida Museum of Natural History team that stumbled across the rodent. He told reporters, "We've really scoured the area and never seen it," further confirming that the litmus test for extinction is not so much whether a species exists, but whether a human has recently encountered one.

• *Indian Forest Owlet.* In November 1996, two Indian forest owlets were photographed by American scientists in a wooded area near Shahad, India. Since there had not been a confirmed sighting of the exotic avians since 1804, they were presumed to be extinct. The U.S. team ran across the pair while seeking to unearth details about a bizarre scandal involving a British bird collector who claimed to have found and stuffed an Indian forest owlet in 1914. Upon close analysis, however, it was determined that he had perpetrated a fraud by heisting an earlier specimen from a British museum and having it restuffed.

"BOY, AM I GLAD TO SEE YOU! I WAS BEGINNING TO THINK I WAS THE LAST OF MY KIND!"

ROTHCO

© Ross/Rothco. Used with permission.

• *Edwards' Pheasant.* In October 1996, Reuters reported that villagers living in Vietnam's Bach Ma National Park had caught both a male and a female Edwards' pheasant. There had been no sightings of the "extinct" bird since the 1920s. A spokesman for the World Wide Fund for Nature was quoted as saying, "Rediscovering this pheasant after 70 years means humankind has a second chance to save this exquisite bird." Hopefully it will happen, but one or more additional specimens will be required, since the female died of injuries sustained during capture and the male suffered a broken leg.

• *Ink Monkey.* In April 1996 Chinese news sources reported that a monkey long thought to be extinct had been rediscovered in the Wuyi Mountains of east China's Fujian Province. The tiny creatures, which weigh only seven ounces and are thought to be highly intelligent, were dubbed ink (or pen) monkeys because, as pets of Chinese scholars (such as the 12th century philosopher Zhu Xi of the Song dynasty), they would grind and prepare ink, pass brushes, turn pages, etc.

Rediscoveries Worldwide

• *Lemur*. Researchers in Germany announced in January 1997 that they had found an "extinct" monkey-like lemur in a remote section of a forest in Madagascar. *Allocebus trichotis*, which weighs less than two pounds, is one of the smallest members of the lemur family.

• *Borneo River Shark*. In early 1997 a Borneo river shark, another supposedly long-extinct species, was netted (with a number of juvenile specimens that were discarded after being photographed by fishermen who did not realize their importance) in the Kinabatangan River in the Malaysian state of Sabah on Borneo Island. In recent years there had been occasional unconfirmed sightings, but the only known specimen was one taken from an unknown river in Borneo more than a century ago and placed on display in a Vienna museum.

• *Black-footed Ferret*. The black-footed ferret was presumed to be extinct after the last known specimen died in captivity in 1979. Two years later, however, one was accidentally rediscovered when a ranch dog in Wyoming returned home with a dead one in its mouth. A small colony of the weasel-like creatures was found nearby. By 1995, breeding programs had swelled its ranks to hundreds of animals at several separate locations.

• *Pygmy Blue-tongue Lizard*. Last sighted in 1959, the pygmy blue-tongue lizard was classified "extinct" until October 1992, when an amateur herpetologist came across a brown snake that had been run over on a road near Burra, 100 miles north of Adelaide, Australia. When he sliced the snake open, he discovered that a recent meal had included a pygmy lizard. Scientists subsequently located a thriving colony of the reptiles nearby and a breeding program was instigated at an Adelaide zoo.

- *Wapiti.* In 1996, numerous herds of wapiti, a species of red deer considered to be extinct since the 1950s, were discovered by Chinese and U.S. scientists on a high plateau in Tibet's remote mountainous region.

Flowers and Fish Resurface

• *Shoshone Pupfish.* The Shoshone pupfish had been listed as extinct since 1966 before resurfacing in its native California hot springs 20 years later.

• *Thin-spined Porcupine.* In December 1993, after being "extinct" for more than three decades, the thin-spined porcupine was rediscovered in the tropical forests of eastern Brazil. Not only had scientists erred by assuming the demise of the species, but they were unable to agree on whether it actually is a porcupine. The nocturnal rodent appears to fall taxonomically somewhere between the porcupine and the spiny rat.

Extinction Happens

Environmentalists know that extinction happens, even without the help of man; if nothing else, they have the dinosaurs and the early mammals to illustrate this fact. But where any modern species of plant or animal are concerned, facts are of minor interest. The environmentalist claim is that they are saving nature from man, but it is also true that they are attempting to save nature from itself. What environmentalists really want is to preserve nature as they found it. They see nature as many of them see economics—a static picture that they can toy with as they see fit—always with predictable outcomes. They refuse to accept the transition that is part of nature.

Robert A. Condry, *Conservative Review*, July/August 1996.

• *Keck's Checkermallow.* This wildflower, not seen in California since 1939, was found a few years ago by a California homebuilder when he and a botanist were inspecting property on which to construct new homes in the foothills southeast of Porterville, California. The weed that no one had believed still existed then served as an excuse to bring the development project to a screeching halt, even though the developer was willing to fence off sufficient acreage to adequately protect it.

• *Autumn Buttercup*. The autumn buttercup is another flower thought to be extinct (none had been sighted for 35 years) until it was rediscovered in the late 1980s during a plant survey in Utah's Sevier River Valley.

• *Ventura Marsh Milkvetch*. According to plant manuals, the Ventura marsh milkvetch had been "presumed extinct" after the last specimen was sighted in 1967. Then [in the summer of 1997] some 400 specimens of the plant were found thriving on shoreline dunes near Mandalay Bay on the Southern California coast.

From the Pending File

There are other "extinct" species that may soon be added to the "Oops!" list. One is the Barbary lion (sometimes called the biblical lion), the near mythical beast whose image is prominently featured in classical and biblical literature (and MGM movies). It was listed as extinct in 1920 after the last known specimen was supposedly shot by a hunter. The Cape lion, a similar subspecies that once flourished elsewhere in Africa and shares many of the regal features of its Barbary cousin, has been "extinct" since 1850. Both cats are distinguished primarily by a long, wide, black mane that extends over the shoulder and reaches under the belly.

In late 1995 a South African veterinarian discovered 11 lions, later confirmed to have belonged to the late Ethiopian emperor Haile Selassie, at an obscure zoo in Addis Ababa during a research expedition. The cats had the unique visual characteristics of Barbary and Cape lions, as did one of the starving animals rescued a few months later by animal rights activists from a circus on the outskirts of Maputo, the capital of Mozambique. Here in the U.S., at least four lions with features distinctive of the Barbary and Cape subspecies have reportedly been located, including one belonging to a couple in Missouri.

Also encouraging is the growing list of alleged sightings in Tennessee of the Eastern cougar. That subspecies has been presumed extinct since last seen in the mid-1970s. Wildlife officials were initially skeptical, but their optimism increased after a telltale paw print was discovered in the mountain ridges near the Alabama border. They believe that two or more Eastern cougars (including a cub) may be roaming the area, perhaps descendants of a small pride observed in the Great Smoky Mountain National Park region in 1975.

Here, too, genetic testing could prove helpful, since it is also possible that the available evidence, including the paw print, may belong to a Florida panther that somehow wandered into Tennessee, or a pet Western cougar released from captivity by someone in Alabama (where exotic animal laws are relatively lenient). Officials hope to eventually find some hair or tissue appropriate for chromosome work.

"Exotics [non-native species] already have been implicated in the loss of more species than climate change or any other human-related factor except perhaps habitat alteration."

The Introduction of Non-Native Species Threatens the Extinction of Native Populations

George Wuerthner

In the following viewpoint, George Wuerthner, wildlife biologist and freelance writer, argues that introducing exotics into an environment—such as the stocking of lakes with non-native trout—often decimates native plant and animal species. Efforts to mitigate the effects of such introductions often meet with resistance from state agencies and local hunting and fishing enthusiasts, he asserts. Wuerthner maintains that exotics represent the most serious environmental consequence of human activity and calls for united efforts to help return ecosystems to their native states.

As you read, consider the following questions:
1. Why, according to Wuerthner, are some people opposed to getting rid of the boars in Great Smoky Mountains National Park?
2. Why are amphibians in California declining, according to the author?
3. Why is Wuerthner concerned about domestic livestock?

Excerpted from "Alien Invasion," by George Wuerthner, *National Parks*, November/December 1996. Reprinted by permission from *National Parks* magazine. Copyright ©1996 by National Parks and Conservation Association.

When an angler caught a mature lake trout in Yellowstone Lake on July 30, 1994, the announcement barely garnered the interest of local media, much less national attention—unlike the large fires that charred and rejuvenated Yellowstone in 1988. Yet the presence of the non-native lake trout in the park's largest water body represents a biological catastrophe.

Scientists fear that the growing population of the aggressive, fish-eating lake trout will lead to the decline—and possibly the collapse—of Yellowstone's famous cutthroat trout. The loss would harm many of the park's cutthroat-dependent species, such as white pelicans, grizzly bears, and bald eagles.

Although National Biological Service aquatic biologist Leo Marnell believes that the introduction of non-native species is an extreme form of environmental terrorism, not everyone shares his view. Even today, the introduction of lake trout into Yellowstone is not universally condemned. Some recreational anglers suggest that the addition of a game fish represents an improvement in the park's fishing opportunities. With such cavalier attitudes, it is no wonder that the growing epidemic of exotic species barely registers as a concern among most park visitors.

Yet alien species are one of the gravest threats to native wildlife and plants. Exotics already have been implicated in the loss of more species than climate change or any other human-related factor except perhaps habitat alteration—to which non-native species invasions are closely linked.

The Cost of Exotics

The growing impact upon global biodiversity is only one cost associated with the spread of exotic species. A large percentage of the expense involved in saving endangered species is a direct consequence of exotic species invasions. More than $1 million has been spent to eliminate non-native brown trout from the upper Kern River system in Sequoia National Park, California, in an effort to re-establish viable populations of the Kern River golden trout—an endangered fish endemic to the Sierra Nevada.

The magnitude of the problem is almost beyond comprehension. According to one report issued in 1993 by the U.S.

Office of Technology Assessment, more than 4,500 non-native species exist in the country. The National Park Service (NPS) is on the front lines in the battle against exotics because of its mandate to preserve and protect native ecosystems and species. Despite the policy, the invasion of alien species has compromised native plant and animal communities in many national parks. For instance, of the 1,000 plant species found in Hawaii Volcanoes National Park, more than 600 are exotic, according to Tim Tunison, acting chief of resources at the park.

The Danger to Plants

The situation at Hawaii Volcanoes is unusual because Hawaii is geologically young and physically isolated, which has created a flora easily invaded by aggressive exotics. But non-native species are a major threat to mainland parks as well. Of the nearly 1,000 species of plants in Redwood National Park in California, about 20 percent are exotic. And Dave Garber, resource scientist for Sequoia and its neighbor Kings Canyon National Park, says a recent survey of the parks' low-elevation blue oak savannas found them to be nearly dominated by alien species.

Infiltration by exotic plant species is often aided by roads and trails. One study of grasslands in Glacier National Park in Montana, reported in the journal *Conservation Biology*, found the number of exotics decreased as one traveled away from roads.

The effect of exotics on native flora can be devastating to entire ecological communities. Fraser fir, a southern Appalachian native, once crowned the higher elevations of Great Smoky Mountains National Park in North Carolina and Tennessee. But an invasion of the balsam wooly aphid, an insect that feeds on juices under the bark, has destroyed nearly all of the park's fir trees. Nothing remains now at higher elevations but "ghost forests"—acres of silver snags—according to Bob Miller, spokesman for the park. With the loss of the Fraser fir, Miller says, another endemic species, the Fraser fir moss spider, is now in danger as well. And the only other high-elevation tree in the park, the mountain ash, is also dying off because of another exotic insect, the mountain ash saw fly.

In the case of the Fraser fir, land management agencies—local, state, and federal—are united in their commitment to preserve the forests. But such cooperation does not always occur. One person's noxious species is another's prize. One example is the feral European wild boar, an exotic species that is widespread in the southern Appalachian Mountains. The boars, by rototilling soils in search of roots and bulbs, destroy plant and animal communities and foster the invasion of alien plants. In addition, these wild pigs consume acorns that would otherwise sustain black bears and deer, eat salamanders and other native vertebrates, and wallow along the banks of small streams, contributing to sedimentation in mountain watersheds.

Exotics Can Devastate Ecosystems

As habitat is reduced, the other three apocalyptic horsemen of extinction—pollution, overharvesting and the introduction of exotic species—come into play. The worst is the last of these. Under certain conditions, a small number of exotic species can alter entire ecosystems and diminish or extinguish indigenous species.

E.O. Wilson, *National Wildlife*, December 1996.

For these reasons and others, Great Smoky Mountains National Park has implemented a wild boar control program. In the mid-1980s, more than 7,000 animals were removed from the park, causing a notable recovery of native flora. Nevertheless, since hunters consider the boar a trophy animal, state wildlife officials negate Park Service efforts by stocking boar on adjacent land.

The Danger to Animals

Stocking fish, a common management practice by state fish and game departments and even once promoted in national parks by the Park Service, is increasingly questioned by enlightened fishery biologists.

Stocking has produced all kinds of problems for aquatic ecosystems. "Many fishless lakes have unique zooplankton communities that have developed in isolation," says aquatic biologist Marnell. "The introduction of fish into those systems has serious consequences for biodiversity, but since you can't deep-fry [microscopic organisms] or hang them over your fireplace, few people worry about the loss of these aquatic species."

In California, declines in amphibians, particularly frogs and toads, are at least partly attributed to the stocking of trout in the formerly fishless lakes of the High Sierra, says Dave Garber, who has studied the issue extensively. Scientists believe introduced fish eat amphibian eggs and tadpoles, causing fragmentation of amphibian populations. The ability of the remaining frog and toad populations to recolonize suitable habitat is significantly reduced, leading to local extirpations.

A less obvious, and therefore more pernicious, threat to biodiversity is the hybridization of related fish species. It poses a serious long-term threat to fish populations throughout the West. Marnell says the native west slope cutthroat in Glacier National Park is threatened by interbreeding with rainbow trout and Yellowstone cutthroat trout stocked in park waters over the years. For the most part, the Park Service has stopped stocking rivers and lakes, but the idea of eradicating non-native sportfish is an issue that most parks have not yet been willing to touch.

Difficult Problem Solving

Problems posed by exotic species can be especially difficult to resolve. Domestic livestock—cattle, sheep, burros, and horses—are among the most widespread exotics in the West. They have had a severe impact on native biodiversity. Domestic animals compete with native species for space, water, and forage and can transmit disease, trample river banks, destroy fragile soil and microbiotic crusts, and help to spread weeds.

At Channel Islands National Park in California, [plans are afoot] to sue NPS for violating environmental laws in its management of Santa Rosa Island. At issue is a cattle ranching and commercial hunting operation—run under a special-use permit granted to the Vail & Vickers Company—that threatens the island's native plants and wildlife. About 5,000 cattle, along with about 3,000 deer and elk, forage on Santa Rosa. Because of overgrazing, 19 native plant species, including five found only on Santa Rosa, are candidates for the federal endangered species list. Grazing also endangers the nests of the threatened western snowy plover.

Despite these and other documented threats, removal of livestock—particularly cattle and sheep—is difficult to accomplish. Recent research conducted in Great Basin National Park in Nevada by independent scientists verified what many had suspected—cattle grazing had resulted in widespread and significant damage to the park's riparian plant communities. Nevertheless, cattle continue to graze in the park because of the significant political influence of the ranching community.

Although typically thought of as a Western problem, livestock can compromise park objectives in the East as well. About 300 cattle graze in the Cades Cove area of Great Smoky Mountains, despite the fact that their presence may jeopardize the success of red wolf recovery. After several cows were killed, NPS recaptured the offending wolves rather than eliminate the cows.

Livestock indirectly promote the spread of other exotic species. The dispersal of the cowbird is almost entirely attributed to the disturbance associated with domestic livestock, says Garber. Cowbirds lay their eggs in other birds' nests, and the unsuspecting hosts rear the aggressive intruder, usually at the expense of their own young.

As their name implies, cowbirds are closely associated with cattle but will also follow pack animals such as horses and mules. The use of pack stock contributes to cowbird nest parasitism in Yosemite, Kings Canyon, and Sequoia national parks in California. And cowbirds are not restricted to grasslands and meadows. Garber says they regularly invade nests of forest-dwelling birds. Not surprisingly, many outfitters and park users, and even some horse-loving park employees, strongly oppose eliminating or even reducing the number of pack animals in these parks.

Exotic species are so troublesome because they are adaptable and have a strong ability to colonize. Most weedy species are habitat generalists that produce prolific seeds or produce numerous progeny. Also, many alien species have ecological traits that make control particularly difficult. . . .

Aggressive Control Needed

Aggressive control can contain or reduce the damage posed by exotic species. For instance, tamarisk, a tree native to the Mediterranean, was originally introduced into the West as a wind break, but it spread readily and now grows throughout many desert regions in the Southwest. The tree not only blocks sunlight from native willow and other species more valuable to wildlife but also transpires enormous quantities of water. In some cases, the tree can draw down the water table so far that springs shrink, reducing water available for wildlife and other plants.

Raymond Styles, chief of resources at Big Bend National Park in Texas, says tamarisk has virtually taken over the park's riparian zone along the Rio Grande. Instead of trying to eradicate tamarisk everywhere in the park, Styles says Big Bend officials take a triage approach. They constantly monitor springs where tamarisk is as yet undetected to maintain them free of seedlings. Where the tree is already well established, but recolonization is unlikely if the plant can be destroyed, the park attempts to eradicate it. The trees are cut with chainsaws, then a tiny amount of herbicide is applied to the wound to kill the roots. Styles says that even though tamarisk suppression is vital to the ecological health of the park, the process is jeopardized by increasing budgetary constraints.

Convincing public officials and land managers to change funding and management priorities to reflect the risk posed by exotic invasions is a challenge facing conservationists. The impoverishment of the world's biota threatens global ecosystems and the Earth's life-support systems. Though National Park Service staff may be on the front lines in the battle against non-native species, they must not, and should not, be working alone.

"A sensible policy would not automatically condemn all foreign plants or animals, but instead judge each on its merits."

The Introduction of Non-Native Species Is Not a Serious Problem

Alston Chase

While experts, including many at the National Park Service, contend that exotic species pose a serious threat to native species, Alston Chase believes that such concern is the product of bad science and bad public policy. In the following viewpoint, Chase contends that defining "exotics" and "natives" is impossible because all organisms move in time and space, hence the policies enforcing such definitions tend to be costly and ineffective. Moreover, Chase argues, some "exotics" actually provide more benefits to the ecosystem than do "natives" and should be allowed to prosper. Alston Chase is a nationally syndicated columnist specializing in environmental issues.

As you read, consider the following questions:
1. What examples does Chase provide to illustrate his contention that some exotics provide more benefits than do native species?
2. According to Chase, what other creatures would be included in the National Park Service's definition of exotics?
3. On what does the author blame ineffective and elastic conservation laws?

Reprinted from "Piscatorial Discrimination," by Alston Chase, *The Washington Times*, July 30, 1995, by permission of Alston Chase and Creators Syndicate, Inc.

A nother wildlife drama is unfolding in Yellowstone National Park. There, rangers have declared war on lake trout, a species hailing from the Midwest, which has taken up residence in Yellowstone Lake without obtaining so much as an entrance pass. This intruder, the Park Service avers, may displace the sanctified native of these waters, the cutthroat trout, and thus deserves eviction.

Piscatorial Discrimination

By practicing this piscatorial discrimination, the service reveals the absurdity lying behind America's preservation policies—namely, the supposition that all creatures should stay where they belong. Uncle Sam not only wastes billions in misguided attempts to save "native" critters that stay put, he also would eliminate upwardly mobile "exotics" that travel.

Since service regulations call for taking steps "up to and including eradication" for "non-native" creatures caught "interfering with natural processes," Yellowstone authorities are also waging war against a gaggle of other immigrants, from leafy spurge to Dalmatian toadflax. In other parks, rangers persecute hosts of creatures that lack green cards, from mountain goats (Olympic Park) and hemlock woolly adelgids (Shenandoah) to Canadian thistle (Mesa Verde).

Meanwhile, the Endangered Species Act motivates federal authorities to disallow stocking game fish, such as bass, when these are thought to threaten imperiled "natives" such as suckers and chub. And countless other laws, including the Surface Mining and Reclamation Act, prohibit sowing exotic plants, even in instances where foreign-born vegetation better protects soil from erosion.

The Benefits of Exotics

These regulations have nothing to do with science or preservation. Rather, they reflect an ideologically based xenophobia that undermines the most concerted preservation efforts. Only after seeking, vainly, to eliminate the newcomer tamarisk from the Grand Canyon, did the Park Service learn that this plant, along with other invading species such as camelthorn and Russian olive, provide vital habitat for an endangered bird, the Bell's vireo.

And in Humboldt County, Calif., conservationists held an annual "Lupine Bash" at the Lanphere-Christensen Dunes Preserve to destroy the yellow bush lupine, deemed exotic, even as down the coast at Monterey, restorationists were planting the same species to save their dunes.

The Problems with Categorization

Such destructive or ludicrous efforts are inevitable, because their goals are indefinable. According to the Park Service, exotics are creatures "that occur as a result of direct or indirect . . . actions by humans"—a criterion that would apply to the bluebird currently nesting in the box nailed to the side of my house, as well as to the squirrels of Central Park and the wolves recently "reintroduced" to Yellowstone.

Similarly, the California Native Plant Society has defined "native" as vegetation resident in California before 1769—which is the horticultural equivalent of saying the only true Americans are those whose ancestors arrived on the Mayflower.

Exotics Are a Fact of Life

Moving other creatures around is a deeply ingrained human habit. Exotics are an ancient and constant cultural effect—a fact of life for the neolithic farmers who watched the spread of Europe's first weeds nearly 10 millennia ago; a fact of life for the people who brought the dingo (*Canis familiaris dingo*) to Australia perhaps 3,000 years later. Some ancient introductions were made over great distances, but the general pattern was a fairly gradual intermingling within regional biotas.

Chris Bright, *World Watch*, July/August 1995.

These definitions fail to note that "exotic" and "native" are relative to time and place. And since all seeds move, what occupies these categories changes over time. For everything that lives is descended from an immigrant. This is called "evolution" and should be welcomed. A sensible policy would not automatically condemn all foreign plants or animals, but instead judge each on its merits. We might seek to control invasive pests wherever their ancestors come from, not replace "exotics" simply because they don't have the right pedigree.

Thus do attitudes toward nature parallel politics. Policies addressing exotics expose a growing—and bipartisan—tendency to confer privileges and punishments to categories rather than to individuals. The U.S. government has become dedicated to categorizing—then rewarding or punishing—all that walks, swims, crawls, oozes or photosynthesizes. Liberals fight for affirmative action, which gives hiring privileges to designated groups. Conservatives, fearing aliens, want stricter immigration laws. And conservation policies divide the plant and animal kingdoms into legals and illegals, bestowing privileges to one and meting onerous penalties on the other.

Changing Values

Yellowstone's trout therefore inadvertently reveal a profound change in values. In the 19th century, Americans sought to improve the Earth. They built dams, irrigated pastures and brought lake trout to the park, along with rainbow and brown trout too, which fishermen still love. But today, policy-makers reveal a reverence for mythical naturalness, which being indefinable, ensures laws are infinitely elastic.

Since "natives" are deemed better than "exotics," this doctrine implies that, say, buffalo are "better" than Aberdeen Angus cattle and since government owns the wildlife, its mission is "higher" than that of private individuals who own domestic stock. This dangerous appeal to metaphysics remains embedded in our laws, where it is ignored by Democratic and Republican reformers alike.

America, the land of immigrants, now embraces policies hostile to foreign species. It declares that plants and animals must not travel. Johnny Appleseed is surely spinning in his grave.

> *"It is the many breeds of domestic livestock—like pigs, cows, and sheep—that are rapidly approaching extinction, creating an economic and social disaster in the making."*

The Extinction of Livestock Breeds Is a Serious Problem

Kelly Luker

Much has been written about the endangerment of species like tigers, gray whales, and the northern spotted owl, yet, according to Kelly Luker in the following viewpoint, ordinary breeds of domestic animals are also at risk of extinction. Luker explains that modern methods of raising livestock threaten our food supply because animals are bred for production traits—such as increased milk production—thereby losing their natural resistance to disease. In addition, if a disease does strike, there will be fewer breeds to compensate if one strain is lost, and whole populations could be quickly wiped out. Kelly Luker is an award-winning contributor to several central California newspapers.

As you read, consider the following questions:
1. According to Luker, when applying an industrial mode to agriculture, what other foodstuffs are in danger of extinction?
2. What is the twofold problem with modern breeding practices, according to Luker?
3. What practice, according to the author, threatens the entire population of domestic turkeys?

Excerpted from "Last Days of the Ark," by Kelly Luker, *Sonoma County Independent*, January 23, 1997. Reprinted with permission.

There is a battle being fought. Although it rarely, if ever, has made the evening news, it is a war that all but a very few are guaranteed to lose. The battlefield? Look no further than your morning breakfast of scrambled eggs, toast, and glass of milk. The conflict rages around the newest eco-buzzword—biodiversity—and who owns God's handiwork. If biotechnical companies continue undeterred, our food sources will be neither God's nor nature's, but the property of Ciba-Geigy, Royal Dutch/Shell, Sandoz, or one of the other half-dozen multinational chemical corporations.

Welcome to the real One World Order.

Home of the Walking Gene Banks

Nestled in the rolling hills a few miles from the Sonoma County coast, the little town of Freestone could be a postcard for rural living. About five miles west of Sebastopol, the handful of homes, volunteer fire department, and country store that compose this village hinges on a two-lane road, generously named "highway," that snakes through the pastures and farms of Sonoma County. The silence is deafening, sometimes punctuated only by the scraws of turkey vultures that glide effortlessly above.

Although Freestone's population hovers around 60, it is still quintessentially Californian, claiming an espresso stand that opens at 6 a.m. and a quaint bed and breakfast. It is also home to the C.S. Fund and its executive director, Martin Teitel. Both are dedicated to prodding an already disaster-numbed world to recognize this latest crisis that threatens our future food supply.

Teitel looks like a man who would be comfortable on a farm, which is a good thing, since that's one of the Fund's many objectives. First, however, explains Teitel as he relaxes in the den of this nondescript building, the Fund is a philanthropic organization of the heirs of C.S. Mott, one of the founders of General Motors. The heirs distribute about $1 million annually to carefully selected organizations dedicated to preserving two ideals held dear by Americans—the environment and the right to dissent. But we are here today to talk about the former cause and what may be Teitel's driving passion—preserving biodiversity.

To that end, his workplace is more than the Fund's office. It is also home to "walking gene banks," as Teitel calls them, livestock that are on the verge of extinction. For Teitel, a philosophy major who has been with the C.S. Fund since 1981, this is much more than a job: it is a calling.

Ordinary but Vital

He lives with his family next door—"a short commute," he laughs—and spends much of his time writing and publicizing his research and concerns about biodiversity. What makes these vanishing breeds on his farm so fascinating is their very ordinariness. As the world focuses on the disappearance of such exotics as the ocelot, elephant, and meercat, it is the many breeds of domestic livestock—like pigs, cows, and sheep—that are rapidly approaching extinction, creating an economic and social disaster in the making.

Teitel will be the first to tell you that people would eventually survive without the meat and dairy products these animals provide. But the critically endangered breeds of goats, sheep, and chickens that live here mirror the story that is unfolding with grains like barley, wheat, and rice—three crops that provide 75 percent of the world's food. Explains Teitel, "For the past 150 years or so, we've applied the industrial mode to agriculture."

Enthusiastic scientists have worked to develop a steady supply of uniform, high-quality goods—large white eggs, lean pork meat, lots of beef on the hoof. One by one, livestock breeds shrink or disappear, no longer needed by a population that they are dependent upon to survive. But Teitel's concerns aren't just nostalgic. The cost of these lost and threatened breeds promises to be devastating.

Frail "Super Producers"

We wander out to the back pasture, where a San Clemente Island goat named Uno frolics with his friend, a more common Alpine breed named Dos. A couple of freckle-faced Navajo-Churros wander up to sniff inquisitively at Teitel's clothes. Bending to scratch the ram between its curling horns, Teitel explains that breeding these creatures is a double-edged sword. Any farmer will tell you that production traits (rapid growth, milk production, and meat conformation) respond quickly to selection pressure, while adaptability traits (reproductive fitness, climate tolerance, and parasite resistance) take a fair while longer. On the road to creating a "super producer," the qualities that makes the animal hardy are bred out, compensated by massive amounts of antibiotics and chemically enhanced feeds to counterbalance its frail constitution.

Now the problem is twofold: not only are animals more susceptible to illness, but there are fewer breeds to rely on if disease wipes out a particular strain.

A Loss to the Human Spirit

"If we lose the sight of the Spanish mustang horse galloping in a sunrise mist, or the sound of a Florida cracker cow lowering to her fifteenth calf, or the tenacity of the Dominique chicken, which has endured for 200 years, we will lose part of our history and our ability to teach it. The human spirit will suffer," says Carolyn Christman, program director of the American Livestock Breeds Conservancy established in 1977 to track the population of rare breeds and encourage people to get involved in raising them.

Karen L. Kirsch and Carole Nicksin, *Country Journal*, March/April 1999.

As an example, Professor Bill Heffernan of the University of Missouri's Department of Rural Sociology, points to the domestic turkey that appears on dinner tables each Thanksgiving. "We found that in 90 to 95 percent of turkeys produced worldwide, the genetic stock comes from one of three breeding stocks," he says. These birds have been genetically altered to create breasts so large (for the favored white meat) that they are unable to breed naturally and must be artificially inseminated. "It's only a matter of time before we end up with some disease that, with this narrow genetic base, we have no resistance to," Heffernan says.

This situation is, of course, not limited to turkeys. Virtually all—95 percent—cows' milk comes from one breed, the Holstein-Friesian. About 60 percent of those dairy cows can be traced to only four breeding lines. And, those morning eggs and sausage? Nine out of 10 eggs come from the White

Leghorn, while 25 to 30 percent of the hogs that provide the "country links" come from only six breeding lines.

Vertical Integration

If the lack of diversity in gene pools is disturbing, to get very nervous one need only look at how just a few corporations own our food supply from pasture to table. Heffernan is especially interested in the growing concentration and control of the food supplies by a few large transnational organizations. He cites disturbing figures: "Three firms mill 80 percent of the flour in North America. Three firms handle the distribution of three-quarters of the grain moved globally. Three firms slaughter about 82 percent of the beef cattle in North America."

Companies achieve dominance by mastering the art of "vertical integration," the attempt to control every aspect of their product, from genesis to distribution. Like the neighborhood drug pusher, these companies develop frail, chemically dependent livestock and crops, and then supply the needed fertilizers and antibiotics to sustain them.

Heffernan points to one of the three major companies that slaughter 80 percent of the cattle in Australia. "Conagra is the world's largest chemical distributor and fertilizers producer," he explains in a soft Midwest twang. "Conagra owns 12,100 barges; 2,000 railroad cars; and 100 grain elevators. They are the fourth largest [poultry] broiler producer." Heffernan sums up: "They control everything . . . all the way from seed to shelf.". . .

Preservation Breeders

The solution for the survival of both flora and fauna—and, ultimately, those that depend on them—is diversity, both of the gene pools and of those that try to claim ownership of them.

Teitel's remote demonstration farm is only one example of what are known as preservation breeders, a network of hobbyists and small farmers throughout the world in organizations such as the American Livestock Breeds Conservancy and Rare Breeds Survival Trust, dedicated to keeping breeds of domestic livestock from disappearing. Besides the Navajo-

Churro sheep (fewer than 5,000 left in the world) and San Clemente goats (fewer than 2,000 remaining), Teitel also raises Delaware chickens and Ossabaw Island pigs, both on the American Livestock Breeds Conservancy's list of critically endangered species.

Like Teitel's organization, the farm at the Institute for Agricultural Biodiversity, an adjunct of Iowa's Luther College, attempts to both preserve breeds and educate the public about biodiversity. Its director, Peter Jorgensen, calls the institute, housed in a 19th-century barn outside of Decorah, "the first museum/zoo to entirely focus on interpreting the genetic revolution."

Cheap Food Policy

The solution to the shrinking diversity in our crops and livestock—and those that attempt to control them, believes Jorgensen—will be found when we start confronting and challenging some of our basic concepts about food, farming, and the economy. "In my view," states Jorgensen, "I don't call what we have in this country a farm policy or agricultural policy—we have a 'cheap food' policy."

He continues, "It doesn't factor in the social or environmental costs. It only looks at how to keep cheap food in the supermarket."

Some nations, however, are finally rebelling against this Wal-Mart approach to keeping our freezers and cupboards full, and which in the process is driving family-owned farms into extinction. Heffernan points to Sweden, which took steps to ban giant livestock containment facilities, such as one in Oklahoma that houses 1 million hogs.

"The [Swedish] government has helped the farmers during the transition," Heffernan notes. "[Now] farmers are making good money off their hogs. [They] produce some of the best pork in Europe, and family farms are being preserved."

Teitel hopes that shoppers begin to question just what their mass-produced, buck-a-quart milk or 59-cents-a-pound broiler is actually costing them—or the next generation. They can vote for change with that most democratic of ballots, he says, the almighty buck. "Shopping is where we can have a direct impact by making choices," Teitel observes. Vote for organic greens, he suggests, or brown eggs instead of white, or meat and produce from family-owned farms.

With what we buy and from whom we buy, believes Teitel, "we can make a direct choice on our future and our children's future."

Periodical Bibliography

The following articles have been selected to supplement the diverse views presented in this chapter. Addresses are provided for periodicals not indexed in the *Readers' Guide to Periodical Literature*, the *Alternative Press Index*, the *Social Sciences Index*, or the *Index to Legal Periodicals and Books*.

Robert A. Condry	"Notes on Saving the Species," *Conservative Review*, July/August 1996. Available from 1307 Dolley Madison Blvd., Room 203, McLean, VA 22101.
Elizabeth G. Daerr	"Taking Root," *National Parks*, May/June 1999.
Mike Holmberg	"Livestock," *Successful Farming*, June 1998.
Kathrin Day Lassila	"The New Suburbanites," *Amicus Journal*, Summer 1999.
Bill McKibben	"Interview with E.O. Wilson," *Audubon*, January/February 1996.
Graeme O'Neill	"Preserving Earth's Dwindling Species," *World Press Review*, October 1999.
Stuart Pimm and John Lawton	"Planning for Biodiversity," *Science*, March 1998.
Kenan Pollack	"It's a Tough World Out There," *U.S. News & World Report*, November 27, 1995.
Jeff Rennicke	"The Long Journey Home," *Backpacker*, May 1999.
Don C. Schmitz and Daniel Simberloff	"Biological Invasions: A Growing Threat," *Issues in Science and Technology*, Summer 1997.
Amy Seidl	"Of Weevils, Thistles, and Biological Control: Is the Introduction of Non-Native Predators a Sustainable Practice?" *Wild Earth*, Fall 1998.
Dan Whipple	"Scientists Claim Future of Earth Depends on Ecosystem Biodiversity," *Insight on the News*, November 1997. Available from 21 Congress St., Salem, MA 01970.

Are Efforts to Preserve Endangered Species Effective?

Chapter Preface

Endangered black-and-white lemurs in captive breeding programs can now be bred without the chest deformity that was responsible for the deaths of countless newborns thanks to the Frozen Zoo. The Frozen Zoo's extensive inventory of ova, semen, and skin samples from endangered species enables scientists to research birth defects, and to artificially inseminate threatened animals.

Many proponents of captive breeding programs argue that managed propagation such as that done with the help of the Frozen Zoo is the only way to save a depleted species from extinction. Jared Diamond, professor of physiology at the University of Cambridge, argues that "there are already many species that survive only because self-sustaining captive populations were established before the animals became extinct in the wild." While proponents of captive breeding generally advocate the release of the offspring to the wild, many recognize that some species whose native ecosystem is being destroyed will one day survive only in zoos.

Many are opposed to captive breeding programs, however, claiming that they involve too small a number of endangered species to preserve biodiversity. Opponents criticize many aspects of the captive breeding process, including zoos, which they claim propagate mostly "cute" animals that appeal to the public but are not necessarily endangered. Opponents also argue that reintroduction of threatened species into their native ecosystems rarely occurs, and when it does, most of the reintroduced animals die. As Barry Kent MacKay, writer for the Animal Protection Institute, warns, captive breeding and reintroduction can be "deleterious to the long-term survival interests of the species" because many captive bred animals lack the genetic variability to resist disease and birth defects.

The Frozen Zoo is the latest high-tech advance in captive breeding and reintroduction efforts. The authors in the following chapter examine captive breeding programs and whether other efforts to preserve endangered species are effective.

> *"Through the Endangered Species Act . . . Congress recognized that . . . we cannot survive unless we take a little better care of the creatures that inhabit the planet with us."*

The Endangered Species Act Is Effective

Robert Kahn

In the following viewpoint, Robert Kahn argues that the Endangered Species Act (ESA) has forced people to view other species as important to human survival and has saved many endangered species from extinction. He maintains that government actions like the ban on DDT that saved the peregrine falcon were imposed in conjunction with the ESA and that other efforts like local habitat conservation plans succeeded due to the requirements of the act. Kahn is an editor for the *San Diego North County Times*.

As you read, consider the following questions:
1. According to Kahn, what species did the DDT ban save?
2. Why won't biological monitors at building sites report illegal activities, according to the author?
3. What happens to the moths, according to the author, when all the jimson weed is killed?

Reprinted from "Landmark Legislation Changed the Way We View Planet Earth," by Robert Kahn, *San Diego North County Times*, January 3, 1999, with permission.

The impact of the Endangered Species Act, signed into law in 1973 by President Richard Nixon, should be measured not just by how many species it saved or how much money it cost developers, but by how it changed the way people think.

Through the Endangered Species Act, the Congress recognized that humans are not alone on the planet, that we cannot survive unless we take a little better care of the creatures that inhabit the planet with us. That may be the greatest revolution in American thought since President Ulysses S. Grant noticed the buffalo were gone and designated Yellowstone the nation's first national park.

Imperfect, but Effective

The act is not perfect, yet diatribes such as Californian congressman Richard Pombo's are counterproductive because Pombo is intellectually dishonest. Pombo claims that not "even one species" has been saved by the act, and that any species that were protected "improved because of actions initiated before the ESA was law or because of actions taken independently of the ESA by state and local government, private property owners and private foundations."

Many actions taken by state and local governments and private property owners, such as local habitat conservation plans, were taken because of requirements of the Endangered Species Act. The act was the culmination of more than a decade of scientific studies that resulted in the ban on [the pesticide] DDT and the rescue of the bald eagle and peregrine falcon. That DDT was banned before the Endangered Species Act was enacted is no argument against the act.

And if a few species were listed in error or confused with other species in being listed—so what? Pombo is not just putting the cart before the horse, he would trash the cart and kill the horse.

Enforcement Is Poor

The fact is, local governments are doing a poor job enforcing the act. Illegal grading is regularly carried out in local business parks and housing tracts, and seldom does a government entity, local or federal, take steps to stop it. The reason is simple: The few qualified monitors of paleontological, cultural and biological resources are the ones qualified to report violators, and they cannot do so at risk of being effectively blacklisted from working again at their profession.

I know a biological monitor who has filed complaints against illegal graders, and who then, reluctantly, declined to file when a violator broke the law again at a new site. You simply cannot do business by suing your employers. Yet with the lax enforcement from municipal, county and state officers, and the grievously underfunded enforcement arm of federal wildlife monitors, private professionals are asked to cut their own throats by helping to enforce federal laws that no one else seems interested in enforcing.

Dodging the Extinction Bullet

In the years since wild creature preservation became the law of the land [under the Endangered Species Act], nearly 1,000 species of animals and plants have been placed on the endangered and threatened lists. More than 40 percent of these are stable or improving, and only seven species have become extinct.

With human help, more than 99 percent of America's struggling species have thus far dodged the extinction bullet.

Gary Turbak, *American Legion Magazine*, September 1997.

The Endangered Species Act was a domestic arm of the Convention on International Trade in Endangered Species, or CITES, a global effort to preserve the flora and fauna of our planet. International cooperation, through CITES, led to the U.S. Wild Bird Conservation Act of 1995, which banned the importation of parrots into the United States—a major step in preserving the species in the wild.

Success Is Hard to Measure

The Puerto Rican parrot was saved from extinction after a lengthy, multifaceted effort that included scientific studies in the wild, habitat protection, nest-building and a nationwide education campaign. Preservation and extinction of species is a complicated event, and Pombo is facile in suggesting that the ESA is worthless because its defenders cannot prove a direct link to the preservation of species in less than a generation—although the Puerto Rican parrot is one such example.

Consider the jimson weed, a plant native to Southern California, also known as datura, or *noctomush* by the local Indians. A few local teen-agers are hospitalized every few years after eating the seeds of the plant, which can cause illness or death, and also have hallucinogenic properties. The plant was revered by local Indians because of its vision-inducing properties, and its use was strictly supervised by elders and holy men of the tribes.

The datura is fertilized by a moth, which also evolved locally. Kill all the jimson weed, and the moths will die. Kill all the moths, and the datura will die. It's a complex, momentous process, and one often jeered at by politicians of Pombo's persuasion, who sneer at efforts to protect a fly, or a mole, or a fish.

The ESA Encourages Science

The Endangered Species Act was a catalyst in encouraging international whaling laws, and in spurring scientific studies of the world's fisheries, which are rapidly being exhausted. The codfish industry of New England is in terrible shape, and Mexican shrimpers say the younger generation of shrimpers is decimating the shrimp population of the Gulf of California by overfishing baby shrimp near the mouth of the Colorado River.

The Endangered Species Act was based on hard science, and continues to encourage science around the world. Efforts to save the spotted owl helped save the Northwest rain forest, which helped preserve the bark of the Pacific yew tree, from which scientists extract tamoxifen, a potent anti-cancer drug. Despite the recent explosion of bio-tech firms, the vast majority of disease-fighting medicines still come from natural sources, as do 100 percent of the flavors of all the foods we eat.

The Endangered Species Act is not perfect. But disingenuous efforts to torpedo it . . . do a disservice to those who would strive to make the act better, and with it, to preserve the precious natural heritage of the only planet we will ever have.

> "The ESA [Endangered Species Act] . . . has
> undoubtedly caused the deliberate
> destruction of millions of . . . endangered
> plants and animals."

The Endangered Species Act Is a Failure

Jeff Jacoby

The Endangered Species Act (ESA) was signed into law by then-president Richard Nixon in 1973 in an effort to save species in danger of extinction. In the following viewpoint, Jeff Jacoby argues that the ESA may have saved a few species, but overall it has led to the destruction of many more. Jacoby maintains that the ESA imposes high economic costs on private property owners by restricting activities like logging and farming if endangered species are found on their land. To counter such costs and restrictions, Jacoby reports that many landowners often kill the animals or destroy their habitat before the government finds them. Jacoby is a syndicated conservative columnist.

As you read, consider the following questions:

1. According to Jacoby, what are the real reasons twenty-nine species may be taken off the endangered species list?
2. What are two of the most significant factors contributing to the recovery of the Aleutian Canada goose, according to the author?
3. How have the private initiatives of the Peregrine Fund and the Nature Conservancy helped conservation efforts, according to Jacoby?

Reprinted from "Endangered Species Act Needs an Overhaul," by Jeff Jacoby, *Conservative Chronicle*, June 3, 1998, by permission of the author.

As the Endangered Species Act marks its 25th anniversary in 1998, the official number of endangered species is near its all-time high. According to the US Fish & Wildlife Service, 1,135 plants and animals are on the brink of extinction. By contrast, only 27 species have been "de-listed"—that is, taken off the list because they are no longer endangered.

The law was enacted with noble motives and high hopes, but it has proved a bust. For 25 years, it has imposed severe controls and prohibitions on any use of any property that might in any way threaten an endangered species. It is a law with such sharp teeth that it has stopped multimillion-dollar construction projects in their tracks to protect the habitat of a tiny fish or little-known weed. Yet after a quarter-century of this relentless protection, more than 97 percent of the endangered-species list is, by the government's own reckoning, endangered.

The ESA Is No Success

Make that 96 percent. Interior Secretary Bruce Babbitt has just proposed de-listing another 29 species. That would leave a mere 1,106 to go. Don't break out the champagne just yet.

There are clearly huge problems with a law that has taken so long to accomplish so little. But rather than acknowledge those problems and try to correct them, Babbitt insists that the ESA is a ringing success.

"We can now finally prove one thing conclusively," he declared in the western Massachusetts town of Gill [in June 1998]. "The Endangered Species Act works. Period."

But as Brian Seasholes of the Competitive Enterprise Institute, a public-policy center in Washington has demonstrated, almost none of the success stories on Babbitt's list are due to the ESA. Most of the 29 species proposed for de-listing, it turns out, (a) were never endangered in the first place, (b) were revived by methods unrelated to the ESA, (c) were resurrected on lands where ESA restrictions don't apply, or (d) are not even valid species!

Take Babbitt's most dramatic example: the bald eagle. When it was listed as endangered in 1974, only 1,600 of the majestic birds were left. Today, there are more than 10,000.

"One of the greatest success stories of the Endangered Species Act," Babbitt cheers.

Untrue. For starters, the number of bald eagles was already on the rise when Congress passed the ESA—the 1,600 flying in 1974 were nearly double the 834 that had existed 10 years earlier.

Moreover, writes Seasholes, it was "the banning of the pesticide DDT in 1972, not the passage of the ESA in 1973, (that) was the most important factor in its resurgence." Bald eagles were dying out because DDT was causing them to lay thin-shelled eggs that broke before hatching. Once DDT was eliminated from the food chain, the birds' eggs reverted to normal—and the populations of eagles soared. The ESA had little if anything to do with it.

Another example: the Aleutian Canada goose. Its population has indeed rebounded, but not because of restrictions

---

How 33 More Species Fell from ESA Grace

On May 5, 1998, Secretary of the Interior Bruce Babbitt announced that an additional 33 species on the Endangered Species list would be considered for removal or delisted to threatened status. Of the 33 species proposed for delisting,

5 of the species are extinct:*
- Guam broadbill
- Mariana mallard
- Oahu tree snail (3 species)

12 are delisted because of faulty or incomplete data:
- Tinian monarch
- Truckee barberry
- Hawaiian hawk
- Chamaesyee skottsbergii
- Dismal Swamp southeastern shrew
- Lloyd's hedgehog cactus
- Tidewater goby
- Running buffalo clover
- Virginia northern flying squirrel
- Virginia round-leaf birch
- Hoover's wooly-star
- Missouri bladder-pod

1 is not being considered by the Fish and Wildlife Service for delisting:
- Pahrump poolfish

---

imposed by the ESA on private landowners. According to Seasholes, the Aleutian goose nests on *federal* property—a National Wildlife Refuge in Alaska. Its numbers started growing when the Fish and Wildlife Service started shooting foxes, a predator. And "the provision of wintering habitat, almost totally by private landowners . . . was the second-most significant factor."

Re-read that last sentence. Time and again, it is *private* initiative that has saved threatened species from extinction or depletion.

The half-million members of Ducks Unlimited, many of them avid duck-hunters, have preserved more than 6 million acres of wetlands in the organization's 60 years. The Peregrine Fund breeds falcons, condors, and other birds of prey for release into the wild. The Nature Conservancy raises and spends hundreds of millions of dollars to purchase land for

---

3 recovered as a result of the banning of the pesticide DDT in 1972:
- American peregrine falcon
- Bald eagle
- Brown pelican

9 exist solely on federal lands and are federally protected:
- Ash Meadows Amargosa pupfish
- Island night lizard
- Ash Meadows plants (3 species)
- Eureka Valley plants (2 species)
- Robbins' cinquefoil
- Heliotrope milk-vetch

And 3 could be conserved by other state and federal wildlife laws:
- Aleutian Canada goose
- Columbian white-tailed deer
- Gray wolf

Note: These five extinct species have been removed from the U.S. Fish and Wildlife Service's list of species on its Web site at: *http://fws.gov/rx9exstaff/delstvnt.html.*

Source: Brian Seasholes, "Information on Babbitt's 'Proof' the Endangered Species Act Works," Competitive Enterprise Institute, Washington D.C., 1998.

Alexander F. Annett, *Heritage Foundation Backgrounder*, November 13, 1998.

---

preservation. Similar cases abound.

What these organizations have in common is a reliance on private initiative and property rights to preserve species and cultivate habitat. They recognize that no one has a greater incentive to be a good steward of nature than those who have the freedom to benefit by it.

The ESA Harms Species

The Endangered Species Act does the reverse: It strips property owners of their rights, punishing them for owning land on which a listed species makes its home. It imposes economic costs so harsh—forcing owners to sacrifice the use of their property without reimbursing them for the loss—that there is no incentive to protect habitat that might nurture those species.

Under ESA, write Joseph Bast, Peter Hill, and Richard Rue in their 1994 book *Eco-Sanity*, the discovery "of an eagle or spotted owl nesting on private land means a forest can no longer be logged, or a house cannot be built, or part of a golf course or campground must be closed. To avoid losing use of a valuable asset, a landowner might be tempted to destroy a nest or even kill an endangered animal. Alternatively, the owner might allow critical habitat to be destroyed by logging or developing as quickly as possible, before anyone else can see and report the protected animal."

The ESA may protect some plants and animals that would otherwise disappear. But it has undoubtedly caused the deliberate destruction of millions of other endangered plants and animals. That is why, after 25 years, 97 percent of the endangered species list remains endangered. The Endangered Species Act manifestly needs an overhaul. Why won't Bruce Babbitt say so?

> "*The revival and survival of biodiversity—the wondrous variety of living things—will require the establishment of a network of large Nature reserves across North America.*"

Wildlife Reserve Networks Are Necessary to Protect Endangered Species

John Terborgh and Michael Soule

The creation of reserve networks throughout North America is vital in order to ward off habitat fragmentation that threatens biodiversity, maintain John Terborgh and Michael Soule in the following viewpoint. The authors argue that wildlife corridors—swaths of protected habitat that link wildlife reserves—are necessary to enable animals to move from one reserve to another to protect biodiversity. Terborgh is professor of environmental science at Duke University. Soule is a research professor in environmental studies at the University of California, Santa Cruz.

As you read, consider the following questions:

1. What is a "reserve network," according to Terborgh and Soule?
2. According to the authors, what is the function of wildlife corridors?
3. What method is being used to study the wanderings and habitats of large mammals, according to the authors?

Excerpted from "Why We Need Megareserves," by John Terborgh and Michael Soule, *Wild Earth*, Spring 1999. Reprinted by permission of Island Press and Alexander Hoyt Associates.

Humans and Nature can coexist, but that coexistence will not come about under present conditions. The revival and survival of biodiversity—the wondrous variety of living things—will require the establishment of a network of large Nature reserves across North America. Large areas managed for biodiversity are needed to ward off a host of ecological pathologies. Through conservation-oriented management of extensive core and multiple-use areas, the vital abiotic and biotic processes that sustain biodiversity can be perpetuated. Outside of biologically viable large reserves, ecological pathologies will continue to spread and take their toll.

Perhaps the most serious ecological pathology affecting Nature in North America is fragmentation. Roads, agricultural lands, and urban expansion fractionate once-continuous natural communities, creating isolated habitat islands surrounded by edges and exposed to a variety of pernicious influences emanating from nearby human settlements. . . .

Cores and Buffer Zones

There is nothing new in principle about the idea of reserve networks. The components already exist in the United States, Canada, and elsewhere. Our definition of a reserve network is a land management unit large enough to contain viable populations (at least several hundred individuals) of all native species. In the Rocky Mountains, grizzly bears and wolverines would set the minimum; in other parts of the country it might be wolves or pumas. The absolute size of reserve networks will vary. What is important is that native species have the space and conditions they need to survive over the long run.

Reserve networks will be designed around core wilderness areas afforded the highest level of protection, where mechanized and extractive activities are excluded. The last and best remaining examples of unspoiled North America should be preserved in cores. Recovered areas will have to serve where large tracts of pristine habitat no longer exist. Many core areas can be designated around existing Wilderness in National Parks, National Forests, Crown lands, BLM [Bureau of Land Management] lands, military reservations, state parks, Nature Conservancy holdings, or private reserves.

Cores will be protected by "buffer zones"—areas to which less stringent conservation criteria apply. Many public lands managed for multiple use can serve as buffers. The purpose of buffers is to shield cores from pernicious external influences, such as alien species, and to expand the area of habitat available to species tolerant of some subsistence or commercial activities, such as light grazing or selective logging. Full implementation of reserves will require reforms in timber and grazing management policies, but such reforms will have to emerge from the political arena and may take time. This is not to say that current policies, however defective, should be an excuse for delay in planning and implementing reserve networks.

Corridors Are Wildlife Thoroughfares

Corridors, or habitat linkages, form the third and last architectural component of reserve networks, linking cores and buffers to one another. The point of corridors is to maintain or restore functional connectivity: to provide thoroughfares for the mobile elements of Nature so that separate cores and buffers do not become demographic and genetic islands. Cor-

Wildlife Reserve Networks

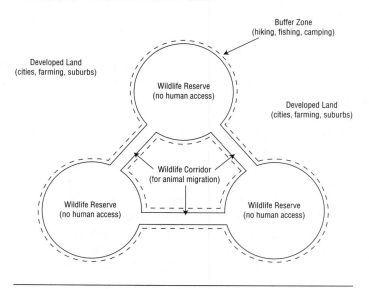

Buffer Zone
(hiking, fishing, camping)

Developed Land
(cities, farming, suburbs)

Wildlife Reserve
(no human access)

Developed Land
(cities, farming, suburbs)

Wildlife Corridor
(for animal migration)

Wildlife Reserve
(no human access)

Wildlife Reserve
(no human access)

ridors may be many things. They might be private ranches with conservation easements, say, to fill the gaps between National Forests and other public lands, so that grizzlies and wolves may enjoy safe passage between secure redoubts. An abandoned railroad right-of-way, given over to Nature, could make a corridor. In the East, even a mosaic of fields and woodlots might serve for the safe passage of certain wide-ranging species. Safe passage is an important criterion in corridor design, so interstate highways and other such impermeable barriers should be avoided or made porous by constructing underpasses, as has been done in Florida, for example, to facilitate movement of Florida panthers.

Corridors are of special importance for the larger members of our fauna. Large animals tend to be rare and often move greater distances than smaller fauna. A single wolf pack may use hundreds of square kilometers, for example, perhaps the size of an entire core. But a wolf pack has only one breeding male and female, so genetically it is but a single pair. So that young wolves may reproduce without inbreeding, they must be able to disperse to the territory of the next pack to find potential mates. To do this, they need corridors through which they can travel without undue risk of meeting trigger-happy hunters, irate sheepherders, or death under an 18-wheeler on the interstate.

All Animals Need Corridors

Corridors are a new concept in conservation biology, and in many respects they are untested. We know, for example, that young wolves have to move to find mates, often over large distances. But we don't know enough about how they move and what kinds of places they prefer or avoid. Several species of large mammals are being studied with radio collars to find out more about their wanderings and what habitats they use at different seasons. Elk migrate seasonally between their high-country summer quarters and valley-floor winter ranges. Many, but not all, elk migrations take place entirely within federal lands in the West. Where elk have to cross private lands, fences and highways can be barriers or sources of mortality. Landowner incentives already exist to reduce such conflicts, and more will be needed.

Smaller creatures may need or require corridors, too, but
on smaller scales. Aquatic turtles are at risk when they have
to cross roads in search of nesting sites. Some species of
snakes concentrate at dens for the winter and then fan out
over thousands of hectares during the summer before re-
turning to the den in the fall. Roads are unkind to snakes,
too. Many butterflies fly in reference to landmarks, following
hedgerows, streams, or forest edges from one patch of suitable habitat to another. Many frogs and some salamanders
migrate seasonally to breeding ponds, dispersing widely at
other times. The needs of all these animals, and many others,
could be served by appropriately designing the landscape. . . .

Mop-up Operations

More than a century ago, our forebears completed the con-
quest of the frontier. For a century and more before that,
they waged war against wild America so successfully that
they almost extinguished it. Mop-up operations against Nature have characterized the 20th century. Now we are seeing
the folly in these past excesses. The loss of wild America di-
minishes our quality of life. How many of us would be

pleased to live in a land without songbirds? In a land without wildflowers? In a land without majestic forests and wind-swept prairies? Wild Nature is worth having because it enriches our lives and nourishes our psyches.

The restoration of wild America can be accomplished through the establishment of a continental system of reserve networks constructed of cores, buffers, and corridors. Reserve networks can be designed in the far North using existing wildlands without the need for major biological restoration. Elsewhere—that is, over most of the continent—wildlands will have to be recreated through a program of adaptive management. The goal is to restore, over large portions of the continent, the abiotic and biotic processes that sustain biodiversity. Essential processes include fire and flooding that shape the physical environment, predation, movements such as migration and dispersal, and others that define the interactions between plants and animals. This restoration implies not merely the qualitative reestablishment of such processes, but the quantitative reinstatement of the homeostatic mechanisms that stabilize natural biotic communities and help them resist invasion by exotics. The recovery of the North American continent (except for parts of northern Canada and Alaska) thus presents major challenges, but challenges that fall largely within current scientific capability. Beyond science, what we need most is the political will to succeed in an exciting venture that will ensure a better future for all.

> *"What science is really showing is that there is no clear evidence that reserves and corridors work or are even needed."*

Wildlife Reserve Networks Are Unnecessary

Environmental Perspectives

Don Loucks of Environmental Perspectives argues in the following viewpoint that the creation of wildlife reserves and linking corridors is based on questionable scientific theories. He maintains that establishing wilderness reserves would displace millions of people, cost them their jobs, and decrease production of agricultural, forest, and mining products; therefore, he asserts, other methods of wildlife management should be considered. Loucks was a Republican candidate for Texas land commissioner in 1996.

As you read, consider the following questions:

1. According to Loucks, how much land area of the forty-eight conterminous United States will be encompassed in reserves and corridors?
2. In the author's opinion, why will Americans have to pay double or triple for products obtained from areas affected by reserves and corridors?
3. What does Loucks recommend as an alternative to reserves and corridors to protect biodiversity?

Excerpted from "Explanation of the Biodiversity Treaty and the Wildlands Project," a report prepared by Environmental Perspectives, Inc., 1999, available at www.donloucks.org/property2.html. Reprinted with permission.

"Conservation must be practiced on a truly grand scale," claims Reed Noss. And grand it is. Taken from the article, "The Wildlands Project: Land Conservation Strategy" in the 1992 special issue of Wild Earth, Noss provides the whopping dimensions of this effort.

Core reserves are wilderness areas that supposedly allow biodiversity to flourish. "It is estimated," claims Noss, "that large carnivores and ungulates require reserves on the scale of 2.5 to 25 million acres. . . . For a minimum viable population of 1,000 [large mammals], the figures would be 242 million acres for grizzly bears, 200 million acres for wolverines, and 100 million acres for wolves. Core reserves should be managed as roadless areas (wilderness). All roads should be permanently closed."

Corridors are "extensions of reserves. . . . Multiple corridors inter-connecting a network of core reserves provide functional redundancy and mitigate against disturbance. . . . Corridors several miles wide are needed if the objective is to maintain resident populations of large carnivores."

Buffer zones should have two or more zones "so that a gradation of use intensity exists from the core reserve to the developed landscape. Inner zones should have low road density (no more than 0.5 mile/square mile) and low-intensity use such as . . . hiking, cross-country skiing, birding, primitive camping, wilderness hunting and fishing, and low-intensity silviculture (light selective cutting)."

Pseudo-Science

While this effort has a noble mission, the implications are staggering. As noted in the June 25, 1993, issue of *Science*, it "is nothing less than the transformation of America to an archipelago of human inhabited islands surrounded by natural areas."

According to the Wildlands Project, "One half of the land area of the 48 conterminous [United] States [will] be encompassed in core [wilderness] reserves and inner corridor zones (essentially extensions of core reserves) within the next few decades. . . . Half of a region in wilderness is a reasonable guess of what it will take to restore viable populations of large carnivores and natural disturbance regimes, assuming that most of the other 50 percent is managed intelligently as buffer zone." If fully implemented, the Convention on Biological Diversity [an international treaty which the United States has not yet ratified] would have to displace millions of people through unacceptable regulations, nationalization of private land, and forcing people to move out of core reserve areas and inner buffer zones. It would seriously reduce the production of agriculture, forest, and mining products. In the process, millions of Americans could lose their jobs. In turn, the resulting scarce resources means the rest of us are going to pay double and triple for these products.

Simulation of the Plan to Protect Biodiversity

The rights of Texans to occupy, develop, improve, or productively use their own property are under siege from a multitude of Federal and United Nations policy initiatives. Under the guise of protecting the environment, wetlands, or endangered species, these initiatives could have the effect of stifling development and reducing property values while failing to materially improve the environmental conditions they are meant to preserve.

Don Loucks, *Environmental Perspectives*, 1999.

This may sound insane, but it's either being planned or implemented right now across America. Land is being condemned or zoned in reserves, corridors or buffer zones under a variety of names to reestablish or protect biodiversity and/or specific species. Should these quasi-religious theories and pseudo-science determine our future?

Reserves and Corridors Do Not Work

What science is really showing is that there is no clear evidence that reserves and corridors work or are even needed. Rather, good forest management, including the use of clear-cutting, enhances biodiversity and sustainability:

• "The theory has not been properly validated and the practical value of biogeographic principles for conservation remains unknown. . . . The theory provides no special insights relevant to conservation." (Zimmerman, B.L. and R.O. Bierregaard. 1986. *Journal of Biogeography* 13:133–143.)

• The theory behind the need for reserves and corridors is being increasingly heavily criticized . . . as inapplicable to most of nature, largely because local population extinction was not demonstrated." (Simberloff, D.J. Farr, J. Cox, and D. Mehlman. 1992. "Movement Corridors: Conservation Bargains or Poor Investment?" *Conservation Biology* 6(4):495.)

• "No unified theory combines genetic, demographic, and other forces threatening small populations, nor is there accord on the relative importance of these threats." (Ibid.)

• "There are still few data, and many widely cited reports are unconvincing. . . . [The theory that reserves and corridors] "facilitate movement is now almost an article of faith." (Ibid.)

• "Studies that have been frequently cited as illustrating corridor use for faunal movement, do not, in fact, provide clear evidence." Of those that do support the need for corridors, wooded fence rows are adequate for many species, while only a few require well-vegetated strips. (Hobbs, R.J. 1992. "The Role of Corridors in Conservation: Solution or Bandwagon?" *Tree* 7(11):389.)

The science used in the Convention on Biological Diversity does not work and may actually reduce biodiversity. The implications of this treaty are enormous and must be thoroughly reviewed before it is considered for ratification.

"Captive breeding is not the ideal solution, . . . but to increasingly beleaguered conservationists, it's looking like the only solution."

Captive Breeding Programs Are Effective

Julianne Couch and Tracey Rembert

Julianne Couch and Tracey Rembert maintain in the following viewpoint that captive breeding programs that result in the reintroduction of species to their native ecosystems have saved many species from extinction. The authors claim that captive breeding programs preserve genetic diversity and have led to restrictions on the use of pesticides and chemicals that threaten species. Rembert is the managing editor of *E/The Environmental Magazine*. Couch writes on environmental issues.

As you read, consider the following questions:
1. How was it discovered that the black-footed ferret was not extinct, according to Couch and Rembert?
2. According to the authors, how was the female cheetah cub named Esperanza bred?
3. In the authors' opinion, what saved the peregrine falcon from extinction?

Reprinted from "Back from the Brink," by Julianne Couch and Tracey Rembert, *E/The Environmental Magazine*, July/August 1996, with permission from *E/The Environmental Magazine*, Subscription Dept.: PO Box 2047, Marion, OH 43306; ph. (815) 734-1242. Subscriptions are $20 per year.

Captive breeding of an endangered species can make the difference between its success or failure. The black-footed ferret, the cheetah, the Wyoming toad and the peregrine falcon have all spent generations in captivity, where they eat, drink, sleep and mate at the direction of biologists. All four have teetered on the edge of extinction but, at least partly as a payoff for "doing time" in captivity, they've dodged the bullet for now.

Ferrets Revive

According to Dr. E. Tom Thorne of the Wyoming Game and Fish Department Research Unit in Laramie, Wyoming, captive breeding of the black-footed ferret was "biologically mandatory" if they were to recover from disease and the decimation of their habitat and food supply.

The black-footed ferret is the only wild example of the genus in North America. It was thought to be extinct until 1981, when a sheepdog surprised wildlife biologists by killing one on a ranch in northwestern Wyoming. Then the chase was on to locate, collar and study the species. The sole surviving colony was discovered in a nearby prairie dog town (whose inhabitants make up close to 90 percent of the ferrets' diet).

The loss of prairie dog towns, caused in great part by farmers and ranchers who consider them a threat to cattle operations, harmed the prairie ecosystem and severely reduced the ferret population. In 1984, there were 129 ferrets in the Wyoming colony. In 1985, a sylvatic plague outbreak caused the number to drop to 58. After efforts to control the plague failed, the population was moved to a Wyoming Game and Fish research unit.

Since then, efforts to breed and release captive-bred ferrets into the wild have been going well. Careful mating has retained 80 percent of wild genetic diversity, and the population expanded to seven zoos nationwide, so that a calamity at one location would not wipe out the species. By 1992, a total of 349 ferrets were being held in locations across the country, and nearly 100 were released into the wild in Wyoming, Montana and South Dakota.

Scientists believe that ferrets have a bright future because every year they have been released into the wild, they have bred.

Domestic and International Success Stories

Wyoming is also the home of the Wyoming toad, which was known to exist only in one small area. To protect it, captive breeding began, and the Environmental Protection Agency (EPA) issued restrictions on the use of 42 pesticides and chemicals in a 100-square-mile radius. Meanwhile, farmers worried that mosquitoes would bring misery to themselves and disease to their livestock formed a task force to protect scheduled malathion spraying. Ultimately, ranchers, environmentalists, biologists and politicians joined together in an effort to find common ground. In a compromise, the EPA lifted its ban on pesticide use, and the residents and ranchers agreed to use a reduced-strength mosquito spray. Meanwhile, the toads are doing well in captive breeding.

Elephant History

Both in Africa and in Asia, elephant numbers are crashing in the wild because of habitat destruction, legalized shooting, and poaching, even in supposedly protected game parks. If developments continue at the present rate, eventually there may be no more African or Asian elephants left in the wild. The only ones in existence would be those in zoos and other captive facilities, and the continuation of tens of millions of years of elephant history would depend on captive breeding.

There are already many species that survive only because self-sustaining captive populations were established before the animals became extinct in the wild. Those species include our own California condor, our black-footed ferret, and our Guam rail, as well as the Arabian oryx, the Przewalski's horse, and the Pere David's deer. Their survival in captivity has bought time during which conservation biologists can try to find, improve, and protect suitable habitat for the species to reestablish a wild population.

Jared Diamond, *Discover*, March 1995.

Some breeding experiments involve international travel. New Mexico's Rio Grande Zoo had a new addition in November: a female cheetah cub named Esperanza. Here's the catch: The cub's parents live on different continents, and have never met.

"The cub is the first surviving offspring of an endangered

species to be conceived using intercontinentally transported cryopreserved sperm," says Dr. Michael Hutchins, director of Conservation and Science for the American Zoo and Aquarium Association (AZA), based in Washington, D.C. Sabie, the cub's mother, was artificially inseminated with sperm collected from a wild male cheetah in Namibia. Frozen using liquid nitrogen, the sperm was then transported to the Rio Grande Zoo, where artificial insemination (AI) took place.

"The cheetah won't breed naturally in lots of cases, so AI has to step in," says Jennifer Buff, a bio-technician with the New Opportunities in Animal Health Science (NOAHS) reproductive group. "In dealing with captive populations, one has to realize that cheetahs suffer an incredible mortality rate in the wild, from predation, disease and hunting."

The AI concept is also being tried on several other threatened and endangered species, including the domestic ferret, tiger, puma, clouded and snow leopard and ocelot.

The Only Solution

Captive breeding has been a tremendous success in the case of the Peregrine falcon. With 39 known pairs in the west and none in the east, 1975 was not a good year for the raptor. But when the cause of the bird's decline was discovered to be a chemical in DDT, the pesticide was banned. The ban, along with captive breeding by the Peregrine Fund, has brought the bird back to viable numbers. They have been "downlisted" from endangered to protected, says Nancy Frueutel, the Peregrine Fund's education director. The release of captive-raised birds has brought the species back to an encouraging 994 pairs in North America.

The Washington-based conservation group Defenders of Wildlife (DOW) is concerned about animals bred in captivity. Heather Weiner, a DOW legislative counsel, says that unless an animal bred in captivity can be returned to a safe environment, these programs create "zoo specimens" that won't survive genetic down-grades.

Captive breeding is not the ideal solution, obviously, but to increasingly beleaguered conservationists, it's looking like the only solution.

"The costs, both financial and to the animals themselves, of captive breeding conservation programmes are astronomically high."

Captive Breeding Programs Are Ineffective

Captive Animal Protection Society

The Captive Animal Protection Society was established in 1957 in Great Britain to protest the use of animals in circuses, zoos, and the entertainment industry. In the following viewpoint, the organization argues that captive breeding and reintroduction programs are ineffective at protecting endangered species. The organization contends that reintroduced animals experience high mortality rates and often introduce diseases into native populations which cause more deaths of endangered species. Conservation programs are more effective than breeding programs at preserving endangered species, the organization maintains, because they protect not just the threatened species but also the ecosystems which they depend upon for survival.

As you read, consider the following questions:

1. According to the Captive Animal Protection Society, what is the highest mortality rate recorded for reintroduced ferrets during the first year of their release?
2. What caused the deaths of forty thousand wild desert tortoises, according to the author?
3. According to the author, what diseases might threaten oryx captive breeding and reintroduction programs?

Reprinted, with permission, from "Zoos: The Conservation Con," at the Captive Animal Protection Society's website: www.caps-uk.dircon.co.uk/zoos/zcon.htm.

"Zoos make much of the tiny numbers of animals reintroduced into the wild, but reintroduction opportunities are nearly always flawed or impractical."

Roger Mugford, Consultant Animal Psychologist to
CAPS [Captive Animal Protection Society].

Of the 5,926 species (mammals, birds, reptiles and others) classified as threatened or endangered by the International Union for the Conservation of Nature, only around 120 species are involved in international zoo breeding programs, and from these just 16 species have been reintroduced to the wild . . . with varying degrees of success. The costs, both financial and to the animals themselves, of captive breeding conservation programmes are astronomically high.

Death Rates Are High

For example, when the black footed ferret was reintroduced to the wild under a programme supervised by the United States Fish and Wildlife Service, the eventual cost was estimated to be around $400,000 per individual survivor! Added to this was the cost in suffering to the animals. Reintroduced ferret populations can experience a mortality rate as high as 90% during the first year of release. And of those reared in indoor cages, up to 91% may die within the first year of release.

In a South American zoo programme, this time involving the golden lion tamarin (a primate), death rates were also high. Of over 100 golden lion tamarins released into the wild, only about 30 survived. While their offspring fared somewhat better, there were other more significant problems for the programme. In 1991 a zoo-bred tamarin, awaiting release to the wild, was found to be carrying the lethal arenavirus. This virus was unknown in the locality and could have devastated the wild population of tamarins and other primate species which would have lacked any immunity to it. The virus may have been spread to the zoo tamarins by mice which they were fed on while in captivity. The infected tamarin had been just 3 days away from release when diagnosed.

During the 1980's, Gopher tortoises were released into the wild in California. A virus present in the tortoises resulted in the deaths of an estimated 40,000 wild desert tortoises.

Arabian oryx were bred in captivity and released into the

wild at an estimated cost of twenty-five million dollars. Recent information received suggests that the animals are again being poached in the wild, ironically to supply zoos. Preventing the loss of oryx is not easy while there is an international demand for captive animals, and the illegal trade can be highly profitable. Since 1996, more than 40 oryx have been smuggled from Oman, to be sold to private zoos and animal collectors.

Protecting Habitat Is More Effective than Captive Breeding

We are, indeed, in the greatest extinction episode since the loss of the dinosaurs, and we are the major causative agent responsible for that hugely accelerated rate of extinction. By far the majority of species involved are precisely those species who do not appear in zoos and are in no way involved in captive breeding programs. Most of the insects and other invertebrates, small fish, and small reptiles and amphibians, shrews and other species facing extinction are generally small and unknown to most people. Many lack English names. Virtually all are dependent upon habitat that is at risk for any of many reasons. An insidious aspect of the current extinction rate is that so much of it involves plants that are the foundations of so many food chains.

Were it possible, there can be no doubt that the high costs inevitably involved in successful captive breeding and release programs would be better spent directly in the protection of habitat.

Barry Kent MacKay, *Animal Issues*, Spring 1999.

In 1990 one of London Zoo's oryx was found to have developed BSE [Bovine Spongiform Encyphalopathy]. The latest research into this disease indicates that it can be passed on from parent to offspring, which raises the worrying question: Could reintroduced oryx have BSE?

Arabian oryx have also been found to have TB [tuberculosis], which can spread between species. In the 1980's the numbers of oryx in a Saudi Arabian captive breeding programme were drastically reduced because of TB.

Trying to restock the wild is costly, flawed and impractical. Animals must be conserved in the wild, thereby protecting not just single species—as practised by zoos—but whole eco-systems. Vast amounts of money—the global zoo budget is thought to be $500 million dollars—are used to keep and breed animals in captivity. This could be used for conservation in the wild, protecting both the animals and their habitat.

Animals Should Be Conserved in the Wild

• Money could be better spent.

• Establishing protected reserves: Animals should be kept as near as possible to their natural habitat.

• Funding anti-poaching patrols: Money is required for even the most basic of equipment such as clothing and transport for wardens, boats, aircraft, fencing etc.

• Education: By educating local people to value and protect their wildlife, and teaching them the importance of conservation.

• Lobbying for legislation to protect wildlife: Wild animals are killed for fur, ivory, horn, body parts for medicines, ornaments and sporting trophies.

Periodical Bibliography

The following articles have been selected to supplement the diverse views presented in this chapter. Addresses are provided for periodicals not indexed in the *Readers' Guide to Periodical Literature*, the *Alternative Press Index*, the *Social Sciences Index*, or the *Index to Legal Periodicals and Books*.

Alexander F. Annett	"Reforming the Endangered Species Act to Protect Species and Property Rights," *Heritage Foundation Backgrounder*, November 13, 1998. Available from 214 Massachusetts Ave. NE, Washington, DC 20002-4999.
Phil Berardeli	"Environmentalists Say 'Hot Spots' Will Make Conservation Easier," *Insight*, March 10, 1997. Available from 3600 New York Ave. NE, Washington, DC 20002.
Jeffrey P. Cohn	"The Return of the Golden Monkey," *Americas*, March/April 1997.
Jared Diamond	"Playing God at the Zoo," *Discover*, March 1995.
Dave Foreman	"Missing Links," *Sierra*, September/October 1995.
Daniel Glick and Adam Rogers	"Lynx to the Past," *Newsweek*, February 15, 1999.
Charles Hirshberg	"Miracle Babies," *Life*, March 1997.
Bruce Lieberman	"Battling to Save Bighorn," *San Diego Union-Tribune*, October 23, 1999.
Barry Kent MacKay	"Captive Breeding: To What Purpose?" *Animal Issues*, Spring 1999. Available from PO Box 22505, Sacramento, CA 95822.
Daniel K. Rosenberg	"Biological Corridors: Form, Function, and Efficacy," *BioScience*, November 1997.
Randy T. Simmons	"The Endangered Species Act: Who's Saving What?" *Independent Review*, Winter 1999. Available from 100 Swan Way, Oakland, CA 94621-1428.
Kelly A. Waples and Clifford S. Stagoll	"Ethical Issues in the Release of Animals from Captivity," *BioScience*, Fall 1997.
Jeff Wheelwright	"Condors: Back from the Brink," *Smithsonian*, May 1997.
Barbara Whitaker	"Released to the Wild, Condors Choose a Nice Peopled Retreat," *Los Angeles Times*, October 2, 1999.

Should Endangered Species Take Priority over Jobs, Development, and Property Rights?

Chapter Preface

The discovery of an endangered species on the site where a hospital was being built in San Bernardino County, California, forced the builders to relocate the hospital at a cost to taxpayers of about $4.5 million. The species responsible for this expensive relocation was the Delhi sands fly, one of over thirty insects protected by the Endangered Species Act (ESA). ESA regulations allow the federal government to restrict activities such as farming or logging that might harm the organism or its habitat, even if the threatened species is on private land.

Many private landowners claim that ESA restrictions on their property result in lost revenue. For example, Ben Cone of North Carolina contends that he lost $1.5 million when the federal government found endangered red-cockaded woodpeckers on his land and prohibited him from harvesting timber on it. Opponents of the ESA maintain that these restrictions take their land from them without compensation, an act that is prohibited by the Fifth Amendment. They argue that financial incentives that induce landowners to protect endangered species are more effective than government regulations.

Proponents of the ESA maintain that only the force of law can make people preserve species, especially when a private landowner's financial gain is at stake. They believe that stewardship of the land is a collective responsibility, so property rights must sometimes be subordinated to the goals of the ESA. Virginia Warner Bodine, contributor to *People's Weekly World*, claims that "the Supreme Court a century ago [established] that 'a government can prevent a property owner from using his property to injure others without having to compensate the owner for the value of the forbidden use.'" Supporters of the act emphasize the vital role that each organism plays in maintaining the ecosystems people depend on for survival.

The Endangered Species Act attempts to save plants and animals that are threatened with extinction. The authors in the following chapter debate whether protecting endangered species should take precedence over jobs and property rights.

"Under the [Endangered Species Act],
federal agents can prohibit you from
farming, building a home, or even clearing
fire breaks on your own land."

Protection of Endangered Species Harms Private Property Owners

Marlo Lewis

In the following viewpoint, Marlo Lewis argues that property rights are the foundation of civil and religious liberty because they prevent outside interference on private land. Lewis maintains that the Endangered Species Act (ESA) is unjust because it undermines property rights by restricting what landowners can and cannot do on their property. Therefore, he contends, the ESA violates the Constitution and religious liberty. Lewis is the executive director of the Competitive Enterprise Institute, a pro-market public interest group dedicated to advancing the principles of free enterprise and limited government.

As you read, consider the following questions:
1. According to Lewis, how do property rights help protect religious liberty?
2. Why isn't Bruce Babbitt following Noah's inspiration, according to the author?
3. How does Lewis define the Golden Rule of democratic politics?

Reprinted from "Noah Was No Bureaucrat," by Marlo Lewis, *CEI Update*, March 1996, by permission of the Competitive Enterprise Institute.

Bringing religious concerns into public life is as old as politics itself. People do not cease having religious convictions when they vote, run for office, oppose or support legislation, and it is silly to demand of believers that they leave God out of their hearts and minds when acting as citizens or officeholders. Indeed, in a nation founded on the proposition that "all men are . . . endowed by their Creator with certain unalienable rights," the faithful need make no apology for participating in politics.

By the same token, however, when people of faith enter the public arena, they have a responsibility to respect the institutions that secure their own freedom as citizens and believers. In particular, they have an obligation to respect property rights.

Private Property Is the Foundation of Liberty

Private property is the institutional foundation of civil and religious liberty. If your home is your castle, then your home can also be your sanctuary (or your political meeting hall). Where property rights to land and other assets are protected, believers can build churches, endow seminaries, establish religious schools—and nobody else may lawfully interfere.

In contrast, where property rights are insecure or nonexistent, the exercise of religion is hostage to the whims of politicians, bureaucrats, or mobs. As the history of the former Soviet Union makes clear, when government owns the printing presses, paper mills, and book stores, just obtaining a Bible can be difficult and dangerous.

What prompts these reflections are efforts by Interior Secretary Bruce Babbitt and a group called the Evangelical Environmental Network to mount a theological defense of the Endangered Species Act. Recalling that Noah was commanded to save every kind of living creature, Babbitt claims the ESA serves a divine purpose: "to protect the whole of creation." Babbitt suggests that only a complete philistine, blind to the reflections of divinity in the works of nature, could possibly oppose the ESA.

What such sermonizing overlooks is that the ESA is unjust and inhumane. The ESA empowers bureaucrats to regulate, and thus effectively "take," private property deemed to be endangered species habitat. Under the ESA, federal agents can prohibit you from farming, building a home, or even clearing fire breaks on your own land; fine you up to $100,000 and/or put you in jail for engaging in the aforesaid activities; and pay you no compensation for the lost value of your land. This violates the Bill of Rights ("nor shall private property be taken for public use without just compensation") *and* the Ten Commandments ("Thou Shalt Not Steal").

"WE CAN NOW PROVE ONE THING CONCLUSIVELY. THE ENDANGERED SPECIES ACT WORKS. PERIOD." INTERIOR SECRETARY BRUCE BABBITT MAY '98

CLOSE-UP VIEW

LONG-RANGE VIEW

PROPERTY RIGHTS

Reprinted by permission of Chuck Asay and Creators Syndicate, Inc.

God in His infinite goodness can bring good even out of evil, said St. Augustine; but when mere mortals use bad means, they usually get bad results. By turning wildlife assets into economic liabilities, the ESA encourages landowners to destroy habitat, even to "shoot, shovel, and shut up." The ESA harms the very species it is supposed to protect.

Babbitt cites Noah as his inspiration, but Noah was no bureaucrat. Noah did not seize anyone's property to build the ark, nor did he tax anyone to finance the operation. The supreme irony is that if Noah were alive today, he would be put in jail under the ESA for capturing and transporting endangered species without government permission.

Religious fervor is no excuse for forgetting the Golden Rule of democratic politics: As you would have your rights be respected, so respect those of others. Wittingly or otherwise, ESA apologists presume that their secular or religious concerns trump the equal rights of other citizens. Such presumption is the opposite of the respect required to maintain civil and religious liberty. Invoking the Bible to defend an unjust and inhumane law should be seen for what it is—a pious fraud.

| *"You mean we actually have to give something up? Yes. The bottom line is that to maintain the splendor and bounty of the living world, we have to change our patterns."*

Private Property Regulation Is Necessary to Save Endangered Species

Douglas Chadwick

In the following viewpoint, Douglas Chadwick argues that individuals must sometimes give up their rights in order to protect the collective good. Although the Endangered Species Act (ESA) requires restrictions on private property use, Chadwick maintains that they are necessary to protect all species, and in turn, human health and well-being. Although the ESA is not perfect, Chadwick claims it will improve as our scientific understanding of ecosystems and biological diversity deepens. Chadwick is a wildlife biologist from Montana and author of several books on endangered species.

As you read, consider the following questions:
1. What, according to Chadwick, makes the ESA the strongest piece of environmental legislation ever fashioned?
2. According to the author, why is each life form important?
3. In Chadwick's opinion, why are small and obscure organisms especially important to protect?

Reprinted from "Strength in Humility," by Douglas Chadwick, *Sierra*, January/February 1996, by permission of *Sierra* magazine via the Copyright Clearance Center.

The rhetoric of most Republican legislators in regard to environmental laws in general and the Endangered Species Act in particular has been packed with references to rights: Individual rights. Property rights. Business owners' rights. God-given rights. Americans' rights. And on and on and on. I'm trying to remember the last time anyone varied this litany with any mention of responsibility. I'm trying to remember if instead of me-my-mine I ever once heard the word ours.

Individual Rights and the Rights of the Citizenry

The social contract in democratic societies has always involved a balance between a person's individual rights and the rights of the citizenry as a whole. (It's what distinguishes self-government from anarchic self-interest.) Boiled down, the Republican argument sounds amazingly like my son's philosophy at age six, when he would pull a face and announce, "I don't like it when somebody tells me what to do." Hey, he had his rights. And I, the equivalent of evil big government, would have to repeat, "Well, there are others in our family and the neighborhood to consider."

As we mature, most of us learn to deal with being told "No" now and then. Others never quite come to terms with the concept. They may have learned that you shouldn't drive drunk, shoot people who annoy you, or pee in the public swimming pool, but among hard-core conservatives, an understanding of civil consensus falls off pretty fast after that.

It's no big deal, say our new congressional leaders, if our common waters become a little dirtier and riskier to the public's health. If the logging and mining industries want a gift of resources from the public's lands, we'll roll back the burdensome regulations preventing that, too. And if a landowner attempting to make a buck causes some little bird to go extinct, what's to discuss? On the one hand, you've got a weed or varmint; on the other, we're talking about a person's right to do whatever he damn well pleases on his land.

Hence the effort in Congress to weaken the Endangered Species Act to the point where the only thing it protects is business as usual. Why? Because the ESA is the single strongest piece of environmental legislation ever fashioned.

It doesn't respond to the usual compromises, nor does it care how much you contributed in the last election. The key to its clout is its insistence on sound scientific knowledge, rather than political rhetoric and economic convenience.

Our Compact with Other Living Things

Where loopholed regulations have failed to protect a stretch of river, the ESA can unmuddy the waters if they are critical habitat to an endangered fish or freshwater mussel. Where the timber industry routinely slips past guidelines intended to prevent excessive roadbuilding and logging on national forests, the ESA can demand a more balanced pattern of use, if that's what is necessary to keep grizzlies or pine martens or, yes, spotted owls in the world. Over the years, the act has become, by default, the most powerful land-use planning tool in America. In places where planning is thought to be a communist plot, it is the only one.

Which is precisely why a lot of folks fiercely resent the act: it is way too serious about its mission. Ever since they realized that not every species could be rescued simply by stuffing a few in some spot nobody wanted anyway or cutting down on the creature's intake of poisons and lead bullets, conservatives have been screaming that America was hornswoggled when it signed onto the ESA. What? You mean we actually have to give something up? Yes. The bottom line is that to maintain the splendor and bounty of the living world, we have to change our patterns a bit rather than insisting that nature always yield first.

The Endangered Species Act is our compact with other living things—a guarantee that we will not knowingly end their existence and that we will actively work to prevent their extinction from non-natural causes. An enlightened expression of our finest values, it represents a stride forward in the moral progress of humankind.

This is why Congress passed the original ESA by nearly unanimous consent in 1973. Liberals and conservatives alike recognized that it was a good and honorable thing to do. The public supported the act then and still overwhelmingly supports it today for the same reason. To argue that any person or enterprise has the right to obliterate a life-form—with its unique genetic inheritance and evolutionary destiny, its intricate role in the functioning of its ecosystem, its unfathomable potential value to medicine, research, and technology, and the pleasure and understanding it may offer to other persons now and in the future—is militantly selfish and spectacularly shortsighted. Not to mention plain old stupid.

The ESA Is Not Perfect

Granted, the ESA is not perfect. There is no reason to expect that we would get all the details of a fundamental realignment between our society and nature correct the first time out. Many conservationists would agree that sometimes-onerous regulations need to be offset by greater incentives for property owners to protect critical habitats on their lands. Most also realize that the emphasis needs to shift away from reacting to crises one species at a time and toward the preventive approach of ecosystem management, which is not only more effective but cheaper all around.

Regulation Is in the Public's Best Interest

The American courts have always recognized that the reasonable regulation of land use is both constitutional and in the public interest. Every day, in every part of the country, city councils and county zoning commissions routinely make land use decisions that affect land value, adding to some land while subtracting from others. . . .

It is undeniable that the Endangered Species Act limits the ability of some landowners in some places to do anything they want—to raze the forest, to bulldoze the habitat, to dry up a stream which contains an endangered species. And after listening to our opponents, I figured there must be some cases of egregious abuse. We went to the Court of Claims, where there are hundreds of "takings" cases of all kinds being filed in waves of protest and you know what we found? In the 20 years of this Act, when we've listed some 800 species, there has not been a single case alleging a taking under the Endangered Species Act. The fact that the Fish and Wildlife Service has never come close to a constitutional taking does not end the matter. The government has a higher obligation to the citizens who elected us than simply staying out of court.

Bruce Babbitt, a speech delivered to the Society of Environmental Journalists, Duke University, October 22, 1993.

Ecosystem management is also a way out of the controversy over protecting the small and obscure organisms that are showing up on the endangered list with greater frequency as habitats are studied in greater detail. Species at the lower trophic levels often play the most significant roles in sustaining a natural community, and are as likely as any others to yield new medicines or crucial technological breakthroughs, but when was the last time you got up early to go out and watch the mites and nematodes? If we take care of the processes that keep ecosystems healthy on a large enough scale, the little life-forms that can't compete in the charisma contest will spare us all kinds of quarrels by quietly taking care of themselves.

Scientific studies continue to reinforce John Muir's observation that everything is connected to everything else—and in more complex ways than anyone could have imagined even a few decades ago. Again, this would seem to argue for conservation on a landscape scale. But, again, the conservatives balk. Moreover, they have worked like demons to sabotage the National Biological Service and its inventory of our biotic resources.

The GOP seems to have dedicated itself to the proposition that, when it comes to biological diversity, knowledge is a dangerous thing. Or, as a six-year-old would put it, "I don't have to learn this stuff if I don't want to." So here we are in 1996, still lacking any comprehensive picture of how our native flora and fauna are distributed, the necessary basis for any sort of ecosystem management. Representative Barbara Cubin (R-Wyo.) says she would like to abolish the National Biological Service and remove all its employees from the federal payroll. Other conservatives would go even further and squelch knowledge already gained; a Republican proposal attached to an Interior Department spending bill seeks to prevent scientists from reporting the results from a study of the Columbia River basin that reveal damage to the habitat of endangered salmon by commercial activities such as logging and grazing.

A true test of the validity of a position is whether its advocates embrace the facts or try to suppress them. If censorship is their ally, they're not worth listening to for another minute.

We can do better, and I imagine we will once this You-can't-make-me-do-it-if-I-don't-want-to tantrum blows over. It is a rare thing when noble human sentiments and scientific data converge as closely as they have in the case of our efforts to save species. There are no real doubts that this is what we need to do, only false doubts cast by hucksters who cannot or will not think beyond the immediate grasp of their fingers. The ESA is the best means yet developed for following such a path. Instead of lashing out at the act, Congress has to be encouraged to strengthen and refine it. It may well be the one thing our generation is fondly remembered for in the future.

| *"The Eastern timber wolf recovery program has taken an enormous toll on the livestock industry and agriculture in general."*

Wolf Reintroduction Threatens Ranchers' Livelihoods

Tom McDonnell

From 1900 to 1930, gray wolves were hunted almost to extinction. With the passage of the Endangered Species Act in 1973, the U.S. government began reintroducing wolves into their native hunting grounds because scientists believed predators like wolves play a key role in ecosystem health. In the following viewpoint, Tom McDonnell, from the American Sheep Industry Association, maintains that wolf reintroduction programs have harmed farmers and ranchers and are actually a way to control land use in undeveloped areas. Furthermore, he asserts, wolves are not endangered.

As you read, consider the following questions:

1. According to McDonnell, how many livestock losses did Minnesota experience in 1989?
2. In the author's opinion, what are the problems with wolf compensation programs?
3. Why does the USFWS want to reduce road density, according to McDonnell?

Excerpted from Tom McDonnell's testimony before the U.S. Senate Committee on Energy and Natural Resources, Subcommittee on Parks, Historic Preservation, and Recreation, May 23, 1995.

If it can be said the bald eagle represents the successes of the Endangered Species Act, then it can also be said that the wolf best represents the Endangered Species Act's failures and abuses. Foremost among these abuses is the fact that the gray wolf is not in danger of extinction. Canadian biologists estimate there are between 45,000 and 60,000 wolves in Canada. Over two thousand gray wolves are found within the continental United States and another 7,000–10,000 gray wolves are found in Alaska. The wolf issue is not about recovery of a threatened species. Nor is this issue about biology. The wolf issue centers around regulatory control of natural resources. The issue also centers around the misguided policies of natural regulation. . . .

The ASI [American Sheep Industry Association] is opposed to wolf repopulation or reintroduction if the recovery program restricts the use of private property or the utilization of public lands by the private sector. We wish to discuss with you the regulatory and predatory effects the wolf has had on the sheep industry. We will focus on the Minnesota wolf recovery plan, as it best demonstrates how other wolf recovery plans such as those for Yellowstone and Central Idaho are likely to affect our industry in the future.

Wolves Kill Livestock

The Eastern Timber Wolf Recovery Program has taken an enormous toll on the livestock industry and agriculture in general in northern Minnesota. According to USDA [U.S. Department of Agriculture] figures, there were 12,230 farms and 91,000 sheep in the Minnesota wolf range in 1979. By 1982 the number of farms in Minnesota wolf range declined 41 percent to 7,200 farms. By 1986 sheep number in Minnesota wolf range declined 82 percent to only 16,000 sheep. This decline in sheep numbers in wolf range occurred when sheep numbers in the rest of the state increased.

Between 1977 and 1986 an average of 234 domestic animals were verified as lost to wolves in Minnesota. From 1987 to 1991 this annual average increased to 1,150 domestic animals, five times the number lost during the previous period. The year 1989 was extremely bad for predation with 1,734 confirmed livestock losses. The state of Minnesota compensated livestock producers $43,644 for their losses to wolves, but by February 1990 the compensation program was broke. The federal government and organizations such as National Wildlife Federation did not provide additional funds to the compensation program and many producers had to wait until the next fiscal year to receive payment. Since 1989, wolf predation levels have remained high.

The increase in predation has occurred as wolves attempt to repopulate the brushy agricultural areas to the south of the recovery area. The impact of this predation has been particularly hard on the individual farmer. For example, Ron Blocks from Itasca County, Minnesota, estimates that he's lost $50,000 in dairy and beef cattle to wolves in the ten year period between 1982 and 1992. According to the USDA Animal Damage Control, a high level of wolf-livestock conflict occurs in parts of Roseau and Kittson Counties which are located outside the wolf recovery areas designated by the USFWS [United States Fish and Wildlife Service]. One Roseau County turkey farmer suffered over $11,988 in damage before the wolves causing the losses could be brought under control. In fiscal year 1992, Wisconsin also began to suffer heavy wolf predation. Douglas, Washburn and Lincoln Counties, lost 111 domestic animals to wolves. . . .

Compensation Programs for Wolf Losses

The Minnesota Department of Agriculture has a compensation program to pay farmers and ranchers for losses caused by wolves. This compensation program, however, is cumbersome, and some farmers don't take the time to use it. All suspected wolf losses must be confirmed by a Natural Resources Conservation officer and payment has been limited to $400 per head of livestock. This payment by no means covers the $1,000 value of a typical cow in today's market and, even if the compensation levels were raised, it is difficult to determine a fair value for the time and energy that ranchers invest in breeding programs to produce quality herds.

The fact that wolves can consume all edible parts of a carcass in a short manner of time is also a problem with the compensation program. If too much of the carcass has been consumed or if decay prohibits identification of cause of death, no payment will be made. Meticulous Canadian studies show that typically only 60 percent of all livestock killed by wolves can be positively identified. Thus, 40 percent of the rancher's losses to wolves are never compensated by the state of Minnesota. . . .

Wolf Is Being Used for Land Control Purposes

The 1991 Eastern Timber Wolf Recovery Program encourages land-use regulations that minimize accessibility and intensive commercial development in the zones designated for recovery. It calls for NEPA [National Environmental Protection Agency] analysis to evaluate the impact of private and federal projects on the wolf. It discourages the building of permanent roads, adverse development, human settlement, and the destruction, disturbance or other adverse modification of habitat that might reduce wolf populations or restrict their recovery.

The USFWS appears to have ignored a 1990 Yale University survey conducted to determine the views which residents of Michigan held about wolf recovery into their state. The majority of residents believed that environmentalists would use the wolf as an excuse to stop development, and the majority of citizens opposed taxes on development or placing limits on human settlement in the Upper Peninsula as ways of supporting the wolf. Few supported road closures and most supported the notion that valuable minerals, if discovered in the Upper Peninsula, should be developed even if it occurred in areas where wolves were located.

Reintroduction Means Land Control

In a rare moment of honesty, Karen Henry of the Wyoming Farm Bureau told the Associated Press, "The issue is not wolves. The issue is control of the land. This [wolf reintroduction] is part of a bigger agenda from the Interior Department to control the West." Wyoming's Gov. Jim Geringer added that the federal wolf program was running roughshod over states' rights, allowing as how he was "personally offended" that Bruce Babbitt carried wolves into Yellowstone (most of which is in Wyoming) without even informing the elected officials of the "host state."

Tom Wolf, "What Price the Howl of the Wolf?" *Los Angeles Times*, February 5, 1995.

In the plan, the USFWS calls for the need for strong regulations. To quote the USFWS, "Because wolves have survived for so long in Minnesota despite bounties and year-around hunting and trapping, there may be a question as to why any restrictions need now be placed on the taking of the wolf." They go on to say, "Widespread industrialization, mineral exploitation, and general development could threaten much of the wolf's remaining range, making regulation increasingly significant to the populations left. Additional roads, railroads, power lines, mines and tourist facilities could further carve up much of northern Minnesota. This would disrupt the natural repopulation of depleted areas by wolves and promote higher human densities which could compete with wolves for their wild prey."

USFWS claims that a road density greater than one road mile/square mile has a negative effect on wolf recovery and the basic breeding unit of the population. In the Eastern Wolf Recovery Program, minimizing road development and road upgrading is emphasized. The USFWS claims that low-standard woods roads have the greatest risk to wolves because they are traveled by hunters and trappers and thus recommends closure and revegetation of many of these roads so road mileage is at or below threshold levels. There is no scientific basis for any of these claims. . . .

A Failed Policy

The problems discussed in this testimony are not unique to the wolf. These same abuses are also found within the recovery efforts associated with the grizzly bear, the bald eagle and the desert tortoise. The American sheep industry has learned some hard lessons about the impacts of wolves on our industry, as seen with the loss of 82 percent of all the sheep and lambs in northern Minnesota.

As stated in the introduction, the gray wolf is neither threatened nor endangered. . . .

Congress needs to realize that natural regulation, as practiced by the National Park Service, is a failed policy that will not be resolved by wolf reintroduction. Natural regulation is not based on science and should not be used to manage federal assets.

> *"Many more sheep die each year because they fall over, can't get up, and consequently starve, than could ever be killed by a hundred or even a thousand wolves."*

Wolf Reintroduction Does Not Threaten Ranchers' Livelihoods

Andre Carothers

In the following viewpoint, Andre Carothers argues that wolves are not a threat to ranchers because wolves do not kill enough livestock to create financial hardships. The hard economic times experienced by ranchers can not be blamed on wolves, he maintains, because ranchers are compensated for livestock that are killed by wolves. However, Carothers asserts, the reintroduction of wolves, while a worthy and noble program, is doomed to fail unless an aggressive effort is made to save the wilderness from development. Carothers is a freelance writer based in Washington, D.C.

As you read, consider the following questions:
1. When, according to Andre Carothers, were most wolves eradicated in Montana, Idaho, and Wyoming?
2. According to the author, how much were Montana ranchers compensated for wolf losses over a ten year period?
3. What do biologists believe is necessary for large predators like wolves to thrive, according to Carothers?

Reprinted from "Will the Wolf Survive?" by Andre Carothers, *E/The Environmental Magazine*, July/August 1995, with permission from *E/The Environmental Magazine*, Subscription Dept.: PO Box 2047, Marion, OH 43306; ph. (815) 734-1242. Subscriptions are $20 per year.

When the first pack of wolves in 60 years was released into Yellowstone Park [in March of 1995], after being corralled by Fish and Wildlife Service experts in Canada, they refused to leave their pens. Smart move. For despite the abundance of deer and elk (the region hasn't seen large predators beyond 300 or so grizzly bears since the 40s), this is extremely hostile territory. The forces opposed to the arrival of Yellowstone's 14 new canine residents—and 15 more recently brought back to central Idaho—are small, but shrill and armed to the teeth: Within a month, one innocent female wolf was killed in Idaho, a bullet through her heart.

Yellowstone wolf restoration is only the most celebrated of a half-dozen wildlife reintroductions unfolding in the United States [in 1995]. Thanks to various state and federal authorities—and usually with the active support of Native American nations—red wolves have a pawhold in North Carolina and a vanished species of bighorn sheep is back in business in the southwest (and Mexican wolves may not be far behind). The gene pool of beleaguered Florida Everglades panthers will be bolstered, it is hoped, when they meet and mate with a pair of mountain lions relocated from Texas.

Ranchers Blame Wolves Unfairly

But Yellowstone has attracted the most attention. By 1940, nearly all of the wolves in Montana, Idaho and Wyoming had been eradicated, victims of a frenzy of killing championed by ranchers, hunters and a government acting on behalf of sheep and cattle interests. Now a majority of people in those states, as well as elsewhere in the United States, want the wolves back. Simple, right? Wrong. Indeed, few federal environmental actions have been preceded by more comments, more discussion and more acrimony—a furor totally out of proportion to the significance of the presence of the wolves themselves.

To summarize: There has never been a documented wolf attack on humans in the United States. The cost to ranchers, in terms of livestock killed, is virtually zero. Many more sheep die each year because they fall over, can't get up, and consequently starve, than could ever be killed by a hundred or even a thousand wolves.

And ranchers who lose livestock are voluntarily compensated by Defenders of Wildlife, which, as it turns out, is hardly a financial burden. Defenders had to pay out a whopping $12,000 in Montana over the last 10 years. Some biologists suspect that the sheep actually will be safer with the wolves around because wolves prey on coyotes.

A Temporary Stay of Execution

So where's the beef? For some ranchers, business isn't so good, despite the millions in taxpayers' money spent on "pest eradication," grazing rights and other public subsidies. In the hands of the hysterical right-wing politicians that grow like nettles in the sagebrush states, this temporary economic dislocation represents an opportunity for demagoguery that rallies supporters, bolsters their political fortunes and, as an unfortunate side effect, leads to dead wolves, threatened and jailed environmentalists and, if you want to take the broad view, the bombing of public buildings in places like Oklahoma City.

The Cost of Doing Business

In effect, the livestock industry has successfully transferred to the general public one of its most basic operational costs: prevention of predator losses. If you raise Christmas trees, part of the cost and risk of doing business is losing a few trees to gypsy moths and ice storms; inherent in the cost of ranching, particularly on public lands, should be the cost and risk of losing livestock to predators. Instead, every year 36 million tax dollars go to kill native predators on our public lands so that private industry can make a profit.

Renee Askins, *Harpers*, April 1995.

Still, reason prevailed in the wolves' case, but it may not be enough. What this lot can't win in the courts, they may gain through other means. According to biologists, large predators need a big enough population and, consequently, enough undivided terrain to remain genetically diverse if they are to thrive over the long term. Eviscerating the Endangered Species Act while turning over federal lands to mining and logging interests means, among other things, less breathing room and a less robust gene pool for grizzlies. It means more contact (and therefore more shootings) between wolves and livestock and wolves and humans. It means an impoverished environment for all Americans.

The restoration of large mammals to their former range in the continental United States is, to my mind, one of the most responsible, thoughtful and, in the best sense of the word, romantic notions this federal government has entertained in recent memory. That it is also the clear will of the people makes it infinitely more satisfying. The wolves are back in Yellowstone, to be sure, and that is a significant victory. But it may be only a temporary stay of extinction. Without an equally aggressive effort to save wilderness from roads, mines and clearcuts, these large mammals will make a brief reappearance, and then they will be gone again.

> *"The ESA protects jobs! It protects people! It protects our quality of life!"*

Listing Salmon as Endangered Protects Jobs

Save Our Wild Salmon

The following viewpoint argues that salmon are endangered due to habitat loss caused by dams, logging, and agriculture. Save Our Wild Salmon—a coalition of commercial fishing associations, recreational fishing groups, fishing businesses, and conservation organizations from across the Northwest—maintains that corporations that benefit from the region's cheap electricity and abundant irrigation water will not support plans to save salmon from extinction without the force of law behind the Endangered Species Act. The economic survival of the region depends upon the survival of the salmon, the organization contends, and thus the ESA will save jobs as it protects species from extinction.

As you read, consider the following questions:

1. How many sockeye salmon returned to the Snake River to spawn in 1994, according to Save Our Wild Salmon?
2. In the author's opinion, how have logging and livestock made it difficult for adult salmon to spawn?
3. According to the author, how many jobs are at stake if salmon are not saved?

Reprinted, with permission, from "Questions and Answers on Salmon and the Endangered Species Act," 1998, on the Save Our Wild Salmon website at www.wildsalmon.org/news/esa2.htm.

How does the Endangered Species Act (ESA) currently protect salmon? The ESA is the law which requires federal action to stop or change activities that cause salmon extinction. It requires federal, state, and local agencies that manage salmon habitat and hydroelectric dams to utilize our resources in a less destructive manner. Currently, the ESA is the reason for the development of a Northwest salmon recovery plan by the National Marine Fisheries Service. It requires that all the causes of salmon mortality [be] addressed.

How does the future of Northwest salmon depend on the ESA? The ESA provides the strongest legal basis requiring government and big business to protect endangered salmon. While there are other state and federal laws which protect salmon and the environment, the ESA contains the strongest enforcement provisions and the legal backbone for a genuine salmon recovery process. Without a strong ESA, powerful special interests, such as the aluminum industry and corporate agriculture concerns, would remain unaccountable for their significant contributions to the decline of salmon.

Salmon a Vital Part of Northwest

Why save wild salmon? Wild salmon populations are declining quickly and if we lose the salmon, we lose a powerful symbol of the Northwest. Salmon form a vital economic base for many communities throughout our region, netting the economy some 60,000 jobs and $1.25 billion annually in income. They are an invaluable part of our region's natural, cultural, and economic heritage, and their loss would be a severe blow to the overall health of the Northwest. Salmon are a fundamental part of the ecosystem in which we live.

Are the numbers of wild salmon really decreasing? Yes. There are a number of reasons, dams being one of the most destructive. For instance, prior to the building of dams, over 8–16 million wild salmon worked their way through the Columbia Basin each year. Today fewer than 300,000 wild salmon swim these waters. Less than 2% of the number of pre-dam wild Columbia Basin salmon make the journey today. Every run of wild Snake River salmon is either endangered or extinct, while dozens of other runs across the Northwest are in dire shape.

Why are the wild salmon dying? The primary reasons are loss of habitat, the lethal gauntlet of dams, and the trucking and barging of young fish. Currently, 5% to 10% of salmon heading upriver die at each dam. Less known is the fact that at least 10% of young salmon perish at every dam they meet as they swim down river. Snake River stocks, for example, are estimated to lose 75% to 95% of their young each year. Also, over fifteen years of taking young salmon out of the water and trucking and barging them to the ocean clearly hasn't helped. Continued reliance on this failed practice has seriously hindered genuine salmon recovery efforts and it's being done at taxpayer expense.

In addition, as habitat disappears, salmon have fewer places to spawn. Logging and livestock grazing practices have increased water temperatures, created silt-clouded streams, and made it difficult for adult salmon to spawn. Although nature is often blamed for salmon loss—floods, droughts, El Nino, etc.—salmon have successfully battled these forces for thousands of years. They are not adapted to fighting impassable dams and streams exposed to silt and high temperatures.

Opponents of Saving the Salmon

Who is opposed to saving the salmon? Essentially those industries that benefit from subsidies. The aluminum and corporate agricultural interests which benefit from cheap electricity and irrigation water do not want to see their subsidies decreased. Navigational barging concerns are also opposed to making the changes salmon need to survive. A salmon recovery plan that doesn't place an inordinate burden on individual rate payers will mean taking a closer look at those special interests that benefit from government subsidies.

Have the politicians who want to reform the ESA expressed a desire to restore salmon without using the ESA? No! Senator Slade Gorton (R-WA) who introduced the ESA reform bill in the Senate has said publicly that we should just let some species of salmon go extinct. In addition, Representative Don Young (R-AK), who is instrumental in the effort to gut the law, does not believe that we should make an effort to preserve Northwest salmon because, according to him, there

Salmon and Steelhead Losses

From 1985 to 1991, total economic output for salmon and steelhead angling in Washington, Oregon, California, and Idaho declined by 46%.

Since 1988, commercial catch levels are down 85%.

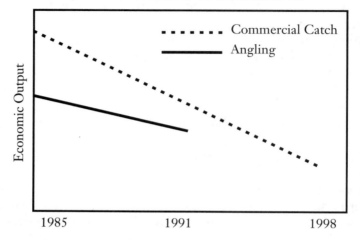

Save Our Wild Salmon, "The Facts Concerning Wild Salmon and Steelhead," 1998.

are still plenty of salmon in Alaska.

Does the ESA protect more than the environment? Yes—The ESA protects jobs! It protects people! It protects our quality of life! Thousands of people who work in salmon-related industries depend on salmon for their livelihoods. The ESA protects their jobs; if we sacrifice salmon a significant part of our regional economy will be lost. The ESA is a safeguard helping to ensure that future generations will inherit a natural world as bountiful as our own.

ESA Is Crucial to Saving the Salmon

Can we save wild salmon without the ESA? Maybe, however it will be more difficult. Politically influential special interests have gone to great lengths to avoid contributing their fair share to salmon restoration, and without the ESA it may ultimately be impossible to get them to do so. We simply do not have the luxury of time when it comes to salmon, and the ESA has set in motion the process we need to save them.

Do we need to eliminate Columbia Basin dams altogether to comply with the ESA and save wild salmon? No. Hydropower and healthy wild salmon runs can coexist. There are currently scenarios, outlined in plans by the Northwest Power Planning Council, tribal and state agencies, and the Save Our Wild Salmon Coalition that would protect the salmon and the billion dollar fishing industry they support, while at the same time allowing continued production of low cost hydropower at the dams.

What do 84% of Northwesterners know that Northwest lawmakers don't? A recent poll commissioned by three public utilities found that 84% of Northwest residents agreed the salmon population will survive "only if we take special steps to protect it." Furthermore, 61% of respondents described the problem of salmon survival as "very serious" or "critical," and 68% indicated that they would accept a $5-a-month increase in electricity bills to help salmon.

Costs of Saving the Salmon

How much will saving the salmon really cost? The Northwest Power Planning Council has estimated approximately $177 million a year and the National Marine Fisheries Service estimates $160 million. This translates into a rate increase of about $3 or $4 per month on an average electricity bill. On the other hand, the BPA [Bonneville Power Administration] and the Direct Service Industries it supports have inflated the numbers to over $320 million a year in order to serve their own purposes. The reality is that saving the salmon will cost hundreds of millions of dollars less than [some sources] would have people believe.

How much could saving the salmon cost me, the average Northwest rate payer? Cost increases to average Northwest residential electricity users would be about $3 a month, far lower than initial estimates. Northwest rate payers have the lowest utilities rates in the country—40% below the national average. Even with a rate increase, Northwest utility rates will still be the lowest in the country. . . .

How much will not saving the salmon cost? Stable and healthy runs of wild salmon are necessary for a stable and healthy salmon industry. No less than 60,000 jobs and $1.25 billion in annual income is at stake. Recreational and commercial fishermen who rely on strong salmon runs are now threatened. Residents of the Northwest in effect receive a second paycheck that comes with living in a vibrant and extraordinary natural environment; the loss of salmon would certainly diminish the value of that benefit.

Furthermore, we have a moral and legal obligation to foster healthy salmon runs for Native American tribes with whom we have signed treaties. Allowing salmon to go extinct would result in costly, permanent reparations to the tribes for the lost economic and cultural value of the fishery.

"Placing salmon on the endangered species list . . . will hang like a hammer over landowners."

Listing Salmon as Endangered Threatens Farmers

Clay Landry

In the following viewpoint, Clay Landry argues that listing salmon as endangered will actually harm them. He maintains that voluntary programs that provide financial incentives for farmers to protect salmon work better than federal regulations that hurt farmers financially. Water markets—the term for the buying and selling of water rights—ensure that there is enough water for salmon and for farmers, he argues. Landry is a research associate at the Political Economy Research Center whose goal is to provide free market solutions to environmental problems.

As you read, consider the following questions:

1. What agencies supported the voluntary salmon recovery program, according to Landry?
2. How has the agricultural community reacted to cutbacks in water rights, according to Landry?
3. According to the author, what were the benefits from the Oregon Trust Lease on Buck Hollow Creek?

Reprinted, by permission of the author, from "Killing Salmon Softly," by Clay Landry, at www.cyberlearn.com/landry.htm.

It's official! Oregon's coho salmon were placed on the endangered species list on August 3, 1998. But the listing won't help to save the salmon; just the opposite, in fact. It threatens Oregon's promising recovery plan for coho, which relies on voluntary restoration efforts by private landowners. And it could fatally damage the growing efforts of environmentalists to protect salmon by water markets.

The ESA Listing Threatens
Voluntary Recovery Plans

Before the listing, Oregon was moving forward with a voluntary salmon recovery plan headed by Oregon Governor John Kitzhaber. The plan had the support of the state government, the National Marine Fisheries Service, Oregon environmentalists, the timber industry, and other landowners. State taxes would raise $20 million (much of it from the timber industry). The money would be used in a variety of ways, from helping landowners protect riparian areas to improving irrigation use.

Many of the participating groups have renewed their commitment to the plan after the listing, and they should be applauded. But the listing jeopardizes the cooperation that is essential to the plan's success. "In terms of people signing on to the Oregon Plan, this will hurt," warns Glen Stonebrink of the Oregon Cattlemen's Association.

The Endangered Species Act listing requires the federal government to come up with regulations to protect coho salmon. But if the federal government decides to require cutbacks in irrigation water in order to keep instream flows high, the result could be conflict, not cooperation. That is what is happening in Oregon's Klamath River basin. There, farmers with water rights face cutbacks in their claims as the Fish and Wildlife Service demands water to protect two listed species of sucker fish. The reaction of the agricultural community has been outrage. Some farmers have threatened violence should their fields run dry.

Cooperative Arrangements Will Save Salmon

It is true that, all too often, Oregon's streams and rivers lack water needed to support fish. But bringing those water levels up to protect fish does not have to involve forcing farmers to reduce their water usage or infringing on their legal rights.

Instead, in a major trend that is occurring throughout the West, environmental groups are buying water and keeping it in the stream. This idea, "water markets to increase instream flows," is catching on in Oregon and is embraced by the Governor's plan. Water markets are based on willing buyers and willing sellers, and they do not rely on regulations. Their success depends critically on the cooperation of landowners.

ESA Sends Shockwaves Through Oregon

The cost to let water run free [in an effort to save salmon under the Endangered Species Act] in Wolf Creek [Oregon] this year: Nim Titcomb's alfalfa field looks like a dying lawn, the lost crops costing him $16,000; Liberty Bell High School's new baseball field is dried-out and useless; and Sun Mountain Resort is delaying a $7 million expansion and 40 new jobs. . . .

Welcome to the Methow Valley, Oregon, where efforts by federal regulators to save spring chinook salmon, steelhead and bull trout via the federal Endangered Species Act are sending shock waves through northern Washington and throughout the rural Northwest.

Peter Sleeth, *The Oregonian*, October 3, 1999.

Indeed, buying water from ranchers and farmers is the most promising way to save endangered fish discovered so far. The Oregon Water Trust initiated this approach in 1994 when it negotiated a lease on Buck Hollow Creek, a steelhead spawning tributary on the Deschutes River. The group struck an agreement with a cattle rancher to increase stream flows in exchange for 76 tons of hay. (This is the amount of hay that the rancher would have grown if he had not left the water to which he was entitled in the stream.) Since this first lease, the trust has negotiated nearly one hundred deals, including donations and purchases.

On an even larger scale, the Environmental Defense Fund has been brokering deals along the Columbia River. In one ingenious agreement, Zach Willey, senior economist for the Environmental Defense Fund, arranged for the Bonneville Power Administration and a number of private power providers in the Pacific Northwest to lease about 50,000 acre-feet of water from Skyline Farms, which had been using the water for irrigation. The deal is one of the largest instream flow leases in the Pacific Northwest.

The ESA Is Noble, but Flawed

Despite the noble goals of the Endangered Species Act, the recovery of the salmon is not going to be accomplished by a wholesale taking of water from farmers. It is going to be accomplished through a system of incentives such as those provided by the Oregon Water Trust and the Environmental Defense Fund. Rare fish will only be saved by people with diverse interests working together, and markets that encourage the type of cooperation needed for long-term recovery.

Placing salmon on the endangered species list thwarts this trend. Federal regulations will hang like a hammer over landowners. If the government can step in and arbitrarily reduce farmers' water usage, the farmers will guard whatever water they have left, regardless of the attractive offers in the market from environmental groups. What is working, "cooperative arrangements that satisfy all parties," will be in serious jeopardy.

Governor Kitzhaber has announced his intentions to appeal the listing. His appeal should be supported. Only voluntary programs and market-based recovery efforts give the coho salmon a fighting chance.

Periodical Bibliography

The following articles have been selected to supplement the diverse views presented in this chapter. Addresses are provided for periodicals not indexed in the *Readers' Guide to Periodical Literature*, the *Alternative Press Index*, the *Social Sciences Index*, or the *Index to Legal Periodicals and Books*.

Pete Bodo	"Wolves' Walk on the Wild Side Proved Deadly," *New York Times*, April 25, 1999.
Robert Bonnie	"Giving Animals 'Safe Harbor,'" *Washington Times*, October 15, 1996.
Sarah DeWeerdt	"Salmon and Suburbs Struggle over a Washington River," *High Country News*, August 30, 1999. Available from 119 Grand Ave., Paonia, CO 81428.
John Gibeaut	"Endangered Again," *ABA Journal*, July 1999. Available from Service Center, 750 N. Lake Shore Dr., Chicago, IL 60611.
Jack Jezreel	"Interview with Wendell Berry," *U.S. Catholic*, June 1999.
Brad Knickerbocker	"Private Property vs. Protection of Species: Two Tales of Taking," *Christian Science Monitor*, March 7, 1995.
Paul Larmer	"Habitat Conservation Plans: Who Wins and Who Loses When Uncle Sam Cuts Deals with Landowners to Protect Endangered Species," *High Country News*, August 4, 1997.
Robert W. Lee	"Attack of the Endangered Species," *New American*, July 1995. Available from 770 Westhill Blvd., Appleton, WI 54914.
Charles C. Mann and Mark L. Plummer	"Empowering Species," *Atlantic Monthly*, February 1995.
Erik Ness	"Taking It All Away: The Private Property Movement Carves Up America," *Progressive*, November 1995.
Roger Schlickeisen	"Wolf Recovery's Significance," *Defenders Magazine*, Winter 1996/97. Available from 1101 14th St. NW, Suite 1400, Washington, DC 20005.
Michael Silverstein	"Market Forces Now Drive the Environmental Steamroller," *Business and Society Review*, Summer 1995. Available from 25-13 Old Kings Highway North, Suite 107, Darien, CT 06820.

CHAPTER 4

How Can Endangered Species Be Protected in Other Countries?

Chapter Preface

The Makah Indians from the United States harpooned a gray whale in the spring of 1999 to help keep their tribal fishing traditions alive. The tribe was able to hunt the whales under an exemption for indigenous people that was included in an international whaling ban imposed in 1986 by the International Whaling Commission (IWC) to protect declining whale populations.

Norway and Japan have continued to whale commercially in spite of the IWC ban with little backlash save from environmentalists like Elaine Robbins. Robbins protests all whaling and points out that "seven of the eight whale species decimated by whaling are still on the Endangered Species List." Those who are opposed only to commercial whaling cite the primary reasons for upholding the whaling ban are the difficulty of counting whales, monitoring whaling vessels, and predicting the environmental impacts of whaling. Some whaling opponents also maintain that all whales are intelligent and sensitive animals deserving of special protection.

Many countries support both indigenous and commercial whaling, however. The Norwegian ministry of foreign affairs claims that "whaling and sealing have always been an important means of livelihood for Norwegian coastal communities." Advocates argue that not all whale species are endangered—for example, the minke whale hunted by Norwegians is not—and those that are not endangered can be hunted in an ecologically sustainable way. David Andrew Price contends that whales are not remarkably intelligent creatures deserving special treatment and claims that "the structure of the whale brain has more in common with that of comparatively primitive mammals such as hedgehogs and bats than with the brains of primates."

"Save the whales," an environmental slogan coined in the 1970s, still resonates today for many people. On the other hand, many whaling proponents like the Makah Indians believe that saving the whales does not have to exclude hunting them. The authors in the following chapter debate how endangered species such as whales can best be protected in other countries.

1

"Because of decades of overhunting, some species of whales and dolphins have been driven to critically low levels."

Commercial Whaling Should Be Banned

World Wildlife Fund

The World Wildlife Fund (WWF) is an organization that attempts to protect endangered species and their environments worldwide. In the following viewpoint, the WWF argues that whale populations are declining despite international efforts to protect them. Some whales are still killed for commercial and scientific purposes, the organization maintains, and human activities such as shipping, fishing, and farming injure or poison great numbers of whales each year. The WWF contends that the moratorium on whaling must be strengthened and more marine areas protected to save the whales.

As you read, consider the following questions:
1. Which countries have killed the most whales since the 1985–86 whaling moratorium went into effect?
2. Why have the people of the Faeroe Islands been warned to restrict their consumption of whale meat?
3. What factors are contributing to the decline of beluga whales in the St. Lawrence River?

Reprinted from "Whales in the Wild," a World Wildlife Fund Species Status Report, 2000, by permission of the World Wildlife Fund.

The tragic decimation of the world's great whales by the whalers of many nations—which reached its worst excesses in the middle years of this century—has at last been curbed. But because of decades of overhunting, some species of whales and dolphins have been driven to critically low levels. Each year over 1,000 whales are still being killed for the commercial market, and the number is steadily increasing. In 1998, whalers in St. Vincent killed a mother humpback whale and her calf, although this is forbidden under International Whaling Commission (IWC) rules.

New and Increasing Threats

All whales face a wide range of new and increasing threats. Today, six out of the eleven great whale species are considered to be endangered or vulnerable even after 30 or more years of "protection" from whaling. Despite a number of conservation victories for the whales—including the moratorium on commercial whaling and the declaration of virtually the whole of the Southern Ocean as a whale sanctuary in 1994—whales are still dying. Since the moratorium came into effect in 1985–1986, over 18,000 whales have been killed, mainly by Russia, Japan, and Norway.

Japan has killed over 3,600 minke whales for so-called scientific purposes, mainly in the Southern Ocean Whale Sanctuary. Norway, which lodged an objection to the moratorium, has killed 146 whales under the guise of science, and hunted for commercial purposes 2,368 whales from a badly depleted population. Norway is now rapidly increasing the number of whales killed each year, in spite of resolutions passed in the IWC urging them to stop.

As a result of centuries of unregulated whaling, the North Atlantic population of gray whales has become extinct, and another is endangered in the North Pacific. The northern right whale is now the most endangered of the large whales, with no evidence of recovery. The blue whale, the largest mammal to have ever lived on Earth, shows no recovery at all in the Southern Hemisphere. Scientists estimate its original numbers in the Southern Hemisphere to be around 250,000, down to as few as 500 today.

The beluga whales of the St. Lawrence river are critically

*"Save the blue whale . . . save the
blue whale . . . save the blue whale . . ."*

endangered, with only around 700 remaining. Like many
other whales and dolphins they are the victims of shipping
disturbance including collisions, noise pollution, habitat
degradation, and above all toxic contaminants. The beluga is
so contaminated by DDT and PCBs that dead carcasses
have to be disposed of as toxic waste.

Pesticides and Driftnets

Pilot whales, still hunted and eaten by the people of the
Faeroe Islands, have such high levels of PCBs, pesticides and
heavy metal that the Faeroese have been warned to restrict
the amount they consume and not eat the whale liver or kid-
ney. Latest research reveals that baleen whales are also affected by chemicals accumulating in their blubber, which
slowly release into their milk when they migrate to winter
calving grounds. Evidence is growing that the effects of in-

dustrial chemicals and pesticide run-offs on whales and dolphins are potentially the gravest threats to their survival.

During the past 25 years, the fishery bycatch problem of driftnets and gillnets has caused the death of thousands, if not millions, of cetaceans. The unusually high bycatch of 128 minke whales by South Korea in 1996 was particularly worrying. However, in some countries today, fishing communities struggle to keep alive the centuries-old tradition of giving whales, dolphins, and other marine mammals which are accidentally killed in fishing nets or which happen tow ash ashore, a human burial. In Japan and Vietnam, temples and shrines built to commemorate the souls of whales drowned in fishing nets are still maintained.

Global concern over ongoing whaling by Japan and Norway continues, and World Wildlife Fund (WWF) . . . is pressuring these nations to abide by the IWC decisions. They are calling on Japan to stop scientific whaling in the Southern Ocean Whale Sanctuary, and for Norway and Russia to withdraw their objections to the moratorium.

WWF is encouraging carefully controlled whale-watching which in 1997 attracted some seven million enthusiasts worldwide and is growing by a dramatic 10 per cent a year in many parts of the world. In 1994 whale-watching generated over US$500 million in revenue. Through support to TRAFFIC [the wildlife trade monitoring program of the WWF], WWF is closely investigating and monitoring the illegal trade in whalemeat.

In order to secure the future of the world's whales, WWF believes that the IWC must regain control over the management of whaling, the moratorium on commercial whaling should not be undermined, international trade in whalemeat should be banned, the Southern Ocean Whale Sanctuary should be strengthened, more whale sanctuaries and marine protected areas created, and marine pollution reduced significantly.

Since WWF's founding in 1961, which coincided with the highest number of whales reported killed—66,909—one of its highest priorities has been to fight . . . for the survival and recovery of the great whales.

> *"The fact that specific whale stocks are endangered is no argument for protecting all whale stocks."*

Commercial Whaling Should Not Be Banned

Halldór Ásgrímsson

Halldór Ásgrímsson is the minister of foreign affairs of Iceland. The following viewpoint is a speech he gave to the International Conference on Whaling in the North Atlantic in 1997, in which he argues that commercial whaling should be permitted. Not all whale species are in danger of extinction, he contends, and those species that are plentiful can be safely hunted because whales are a renewable resource. Ásgrímsson maintains that hunting should be permitted because many nations depend on marine resources like the whale for survival and have historically managed these resources wisely.

As you read, consider the following questions:
1. Of the many groups with views on commercial whaling, which one does Ásgrímsson believe is smallest?
2. According to Ásgrímsson, what percentage of Iceland's total export earnings come from marine products?
3. What argument does the author make using cod as an example?

Excerpted from the opening address of Halldór Ásgrímsson to the International Conference on Whaling in the North Atlantic: Economic and Political Perspectives, Reykjavík, Iceland, March 1, 1997.

[In 1992], I left my post as Minister of Fisheries after having held that position in the Government of Iceland for nearly 8 years. During that period, a considerable part of my time and energy was devoted to the whaling question. I participated in some of the meetings of the International Whaling Commission [and] made several trips to neighbouring countries to consult and negotiate the issue. In all modesty I think I can claim to have been one of the principal players in strengthening the cooperation of countries in the high north, which led to the establishment of the North Atlantic Marine Mammal Commission (NAMMCO).

Different Views on Whaling

All this came about because in the last 25 years or so, quite different views on the whale stocks and their utilization have evolved.

First, we have the view of those who regard the whale stocks as a renewable, exploitable resource and favour scientifically based, sustainable harvesting of this resource.

Secondly, there are those who are not willing to accept the view that whales are an exploitable resource and are convinced that whales are special animals that deserve full protection. The anti-whaling industry, which often claims this view, has in fact become a regular business in its own right, fuelled by well meaning, innocent people who donate their money to something they believe will improve our world.

The third category consists of those who in general agree that whales are an exploitable resource but think that stronger scientific evidence on the status of the stocks is still needed.

In my opinion the second group, the fanatics, is the smallest, while I think the last mentioned group, people with a more reasonable approach to the whaling question, but who are perhaps not well informed, deserve more attention. I have to admit that we have not done enough to provide information in recent years and that we still have much work ahead.

Plenty of Whales

Icelanders depend for their livelihood on the sea and its resources: the seafood. Marine products account for almost 80% of Iceland's total export earnings. Our waters are among the richest fishing grounds in the world, and we have done our utmost to conserve the fish stocks and increase their utilization. To do so we have applied extensive marine research programmes and the best available scientific methodology.

A Case for Whaleburgers

Over the past twenty years, the save-the-whales movement has been so successful in shaping public sentiment about the whaling industry that the U.S. and other nations have adopted a worldwide moratorium on whaling. Part of the credit must go to the animals themselves, which are more charismatic on television than Kurds, Bosnians, or Rwandans, who have engendered far less international protection. The movement owes most of its success, however, to the gullibility of Hollywood and the press in passing along bogus claims from whaling's opponents.

The mainstay of the case against whaling—that it threatens an endangered species—is characteristic of the misinformation. It is true that European nations and the United States killed enormous numbers of whales during commercial whaling's heyday in the nineteenth century, but to say that "whales" are endangered is no more meaningful than to say that "birds" are endangered; there are more than seventy species of whales, and their numbers vary dramatically. Some are endangered, some are not. . . .

The only whale species that . . . Norwegian whalers hunt is the minke, which Norwegians eat as whale steaks, whale meatballs, and whaleburgers. As it turns out, minke whales are no more in danger of extinction than Angus cattle.

David Andrew Price, *American Spectator*, Fall 1995.

In our view, we should apply the same methods to marine mammals. Investigations by the Scientific Committee of the IWC, and later by the Scientific Committee of NAMMCO have indeed shown that the stocks of minke, fin and sei whales in the North Atlantic are well above harvestable levels.

Although today it is undeniable that certain whale stocks can be safely harvested, widespread and vocal calls are being made for complete protection of all whales, regardless of the state of specific stocks. These demands have been supported by various nations, particularly in the western world.

It is understandable that environmental campaigners

should focus on endangered species, and it is also understandable that their arguments about whales should appeal to nations that have little acquaintance with fisheries. But bracketing all species of the same biological order together as far as utilization is concerned is clearly out of the question for communities of the high north, largely dependent on the marine resources. No one would consider, for example, enforcing a worldwide ban on fishing only because the cod population on certain banks has been endangered by overfishing. Exactly the same principle applies to marine mammals, the fact that specific whale stocks are endangered is no argument for protecting all whale stocks.

Whales Are Resources

Unqualified protection of all whales and other marine mammals is also contrary to modern concepts of sustainable resource management. The 1992 United Nations Conference on the Environment and Development (UNCED) in Rio de Janeiro endorsed the basic principle that all states should commit themselves to the conservation and sustainable use of living marine resources. Nations that bear the greatest responsibility for rational utilization of marine resources cannot, therefore, accept the notion of total protection of whales.

The Rio Conference endorsed the right of states to utilize their own resources in accordance with their own environmental and development strategies. Prior to that, the United Nations Convention on the Law of the Sea acknowledged the jurisdiction of states over such utilization within their 200-mile exclusive economic zones. It also recognized marine mammals as a resource, and declared that states should cooperate with a view to the conservation of cetaceans through the appropriate international organizations for their conservation, management and study. Iceland has met its obligations in this area and will continue to do so. With respect to the International Whaling Commission, Iceland is understandably very reluctant to rejoin, as the Commission has failed to adhere to its own convention.

Ladies and gentlemen, clearly, international law and science as well as the modern philosophy of sustainable development are in favour of rational utilization of the resources.

All responsible nations must utilize their resources with both the interests of present and future generations in mind. Coastal states with centuries of fishing experience ought to have developed the most reliable knowledge about the best way to harvest these resources.

Iceland's viewpoint has thus been, and still is, that safe harvesting of the whale stocks under active supervision and based on [a] scientific foundation offers an economical and sustainable way of utilizing the resources of the ocean. We need to carry that message forward before it becomes history to catch whales (or even fish for that matter). It is important that countries in the north speak with one voice on this issue. Only then will we be able to establish a more tolerant view towards our value judgements and cultures, which indeed is a key to the solution of this issue.

> "*Observing the hunters, though, you get the impression they think that whole extinction business was all nonsense. As if the elephants were just getting better at hiding.*"

Elephant Hunting Should Be Banned

Matthew Scully

In the following viewpoint, Matthew Scully argues that making elephants available and lucrative to hunt will not save them from extinction. He maintains that hunting safari outfitters do not provide economic benefits to the local people or, as claimed, to the elephants. Scully calls for more aid to Africa to support nonhunting industries and a U.S. ban on the importation of all elephant products. Scully, a speechwriter for the Bush administration, is now a freelance writer.

As you read, consider the following questions:
1. What is "Campfire," according to Scully?
2. Why is the hunting good in Zimbabwe, according to the website that Scully cites?
3. According to the author, how old is the average adult elephant now and how old did the average adult used to be?

You'd think that after a century's worth of service as the noble Republican symbol, the elephant might enjoy some special conservation status in the party. But it was a Democrat, Senator Barbara Boxer of California, who rose [in 1997] in its defense.

By voice vote, the Senate approved her motion to restrict American financing for Campfire, a program in Zimbabwe under which elephant hunting is allowed as a means of raising local revenue.

By the logic of Campfire, the only way to save the elephant is to turn him over to the hunter. Around the world are hunters willing to pay good money for an elephant. Surrounding the elephant preserves are poor communities that could certainly use the revenue. So, the argument runs, give those communities control over elephants, and let them sell the hunting rights at premium rates. They will thus have an incentive to guard against poachers. From now on, only paying customers get to hunt.

The idea of trophy hunters as the elephant's only deliverance from poachers may not sit well with some of us, but such is life. Best, we're told, to avert our eyes and let Market Forces work another miracle. Campfire, as one proponent put it in the *Weekly Standard*, has "transformed elephants from economic liabilities into community assets," thereby "empowering the peasants."

The economics do seem to add up, but one thing I notice in all these arguments is that 'we never meet the Market Force himself, the trophy hunter upon whose money and conservation instincts the whole plan rests. To see how Campfire is playing out on the consumer end, go on line sometime, key in "hunting" and "elephant" and you'll find dozens of safari outfitters advertising what looks to be a trophy free-for-all. "Come to Tanzania," says one company, "the very essence of Africa, unspoiled yet spectacular." The "Big Four"—elephants, lions, leopards, buffalo—are all there. And best of all, "You may shoot as much as you please."

Internet Insight into Trophy Hunting Culture

Come to Zimbabwe, beckons Matupula Hunters of Texas, for "Africa's best elephant hunting." And hurry: "With the country dry and surface water limited, the elephant bulls can be tracked going to and from water, or in amongst the woodlands and forest where they feed and lay up."

Let me explain: It's hot and dry. The creatures live in a fenced game park where water is scarce. Though wary of the water hole, they have to drink sometime, and when they do you'll be positioned just right. Catching them en route makes for "an exciting and rewarding elephant hunt."

"IT'S REALLY BETTER THIS WAY. AT THE MOST, I'LL GET MUGGED."

David Catrow. Reprinted by permission of Copley News Service.

A few restrictions still apply. "No Elephants are allowed to be hunted in Mozambique," says Hunt Mozambique Inc. You can stay for that tempting "Lion and Buffalo Package" ($13,450) or head over to Zimbabwe where the action is. Daily rates there cover "accommodation in fully equipped tented safari camp, camp personnel, all meals, daily laundry service, trackers and skinners, field preparation of trophies, vehicle transport during hunt, services of PH"—professional hunter. With Dembe Safaris you'll have a hunt "reminiscent of Hemingway," unless you prefer "luxurious 5-star lodges with swimming pools, TV, and all the amenities."

But for skinner and PH, one notices, all these are things a tourist armed only with camera would pay for, which makes you wonder why nonhunting tourism (let alone nontourism trades) could not just as well support those communities. On the other hand, then we could not don safari suits and feel like Hemingway. We would miss the rewarding experience of being fed, tidied up, tucked in, served breakfast, driven up to a trapped and thirsty animal—on his best day, about as hard to hit as Bullwinkle floating down Fifth Avenue—and after our kill repairing to the hotel bar to swap stories, while the empowered peasants handle the skinning and stuffing back in the bush.

Adventures Unlimited lays down what seems to be the standard rule: "Trophy fees payable when animals are killed or wounded." The fees: "Elephant—$10,000; Giraffe—$1,000; Lion—$3,500; Hippo—$2,500." At just $700 the zebras are a steal, and for $75 you can shoot yourself some "Bait"—an impala.

There are pictures, too. A client of Adventures Unlimited, a meager fellow bearing some serious weaponry, grins at us through the now horizontal tusks of an elephant that has just been transformed into a community asset. The great elephant, all $10,000 worth, looks asleep.

Oh, and you can also enjoy vicarious adventures through videos like "Pure Africa" ("lots of action and kill shots"), "Sudden Death" ("wounded trophy lions") or, for the gals, "Lady Africa."

There are now 500,000 or so elephants left across the continent, down from roughly 1.3 million in 1979. Your average adult is maybe 20 years old. It used to be around 60. All but a few of the trophy-ready elders have assumed their places in living rooms and lodges across the Western world. Observing the hunters, though, you get the impression they think that whole extinction business was all nonsense. As if the elephants were just getting better at hiding.

Having spent a few generations exploiting Africa, without much apparent concern for "community development," the hunters now offer themselves as a free-market solution. Actually, the arrangement more resembles a monopoly, the ivory and hunting industries buying off the locals and agreeing with each other to "leave enough for us!"

Senator Boxer's proposal on Campfire—an amendment to

an appropriation bill for foreign operations—[went] before the House. [At press time, the bill had not passed.] She and Senator Wayne Allard of Colorado, the most vocal Republican on the issue, are right to oppose Campfire, but don't stop there. Redouble aid to Africa and see that every dollar goes to building nonhunting industries. Offer every tax incentive in the book for investment in Africa, including a deduction for dollars spent there by unarmed tourists. And ban the importation of any elephant trophy across American borders—providing violators with fresh attire, trained escort and vehicle transport on their one-year prison adventure, all amenities included.

| *"Zimbabwe is using hunting to check the surging elephant population, enhance wildlife habitat and enable villagers and elephants to live in harmony."*

Elephant Hunting Should Not Be Banned

Richard Miniter

In the following viewpoint, Richard Miniter argues that elephants are overpopulated in Zimbabwe and claims they are destroying the habitats that they share with other species, consuming croplands that villagers depend on for survival, and killing local people. He contends that hunting elephants maintains sustainable elephant populations and that the hunting fees provide local people with money for needed projects and conservation programs. Richard Miniter, who has written about environmental issues for more than a decade, writes for the *Wall Street Journal*, *Reader's Digest*, the *Atlantic Monthly*, and other publications. He can be reached at rminiter@aol.com.

As you read, consider the following questions:
1. How many trees per day does an elephant knock down, according to Miniter?
2. According to the author, how much cropland can one elephant herd consume in an evening?
3. On what does the Zimbabwe National Parks and Wildlife Department spend hunting revenues, according to the author?

Hwange National Park, Zimbabwe—Several hours northeast of Bulawayo, Zimbabwe's second-largest city, the road turns to sand and you arrive in elephant country. This park is home to one of Africa's largest elephant herds—and to scenes of elephantine destruction.

Elephantine Destruction

Inside the park, hungry elephants busily strip trees of their low-hanging leaves, then push them down and devour their tops. Nearby lies a water hole drained by elephants and befouled by heaps of their dung. Antelopes and other wildlife wander across the muddy hole, hoping to find a small puddle to drink from. Today they are disappointed.

A single elephant knocks down 1,500 trees per year and drinks 13 gallons of water per day. Soon smaller animals, deprived of shade and water, will be forced to flee the park as elephants trample Zimbabwe's distinctive grasslands into deserts. For years environmentalists have asked us to imagine a world without elephants; in Hwange we see the dire effect of too many.

Half a world away, Sen. Barbara Boxer (D., Calif.), who hopes to end elephant hunting, is leading an effort to cut off U.S. funds for Campfire, an innovative Zimbabwean program that shares hunting revenues with villagers and wildlife officials. Ms. Boxer's effort is misguided: Overpopulation, not overhunting, is a serious problem. The Kalahari Desert can feed one elephant per square kilometer; it now supports twice that. And overcrowding will surely worsen: Zimbabwe's elephant population (currently estimated at 66,500) is growing by 5% per year.

Elephant Overpopulation

Elephant overpopulation is a threat to other species and to the environment. "If the elephant population is not controlled, there will be no grazing for other animals, and those animals will die," explains Matusadona National Park warden Zephania Muketiwa, as he approaches one of the world's few remaining black rhinos.

Elephant overpopulation also threatens human lives and livelihoods. Villagers in Tsholotsho's Rural District No. 7 are still talking about Ndwandwe Ndlovu, who was trampled to death by elephants in 1995. (Ironically, his surname means "elephant.") Further north, more than 100 people have been killed by elephants in the Zambezi valley since 1980.

Hunting Provides the Incentive to Protect Elephants

The greatest threats to elephants is habitat loss. Making them less valuable [by prohibiting hunters from hunting them] may discourage some poaching, but by encouraging habitat destruction, this devaluation has surely harmed elephant populations. Countries like Zimbabwe with its CAMPFIRE program are realizing that the greatest incentive to protect habitat comes from allowing local people to benefit from the wildlife that surrounds them. In this case, devaluing elephants only means less effort will be put into providing space for them.

Michael De Alessi, *CEI Update*, August 1997.

More common is elephant destruction of crops, fences and buildings, especially granaries. Jack Mthembo, Tsholotsho's Rural District Council chairman, points at a map that shows that more than 200 cornfields have been devoured by elephants in the past year. One elephant herd consumes nearly 10 acres of cropland in an evening—often the annual food supply for an entire family.

Hunting Saves Elephants

Without hunting, wildlife managers have two alternatives: do nothing and allow elephants to die from starvation (as they did in Gonarezhou National Park in 1992), or employ park rangers to kill selected elephants, an unpleasant and expensive task that takes money from other wildlife protection measures. Either way, elephants will die. A better alternative, as the World Wildlife Fund and the African Wildlife Foundation both acknowledge, is for the government to sell hunting licenses to support conservation and development.

The good hunting can do is evident in Tsholotsho, where villages receive 60% of hunting license fees through Campfire. They use the funds to build elephant-proof electric fences or to compensate the victims of elephants. Hunting revenues have changed the attitudes of villagers. "Since the introduction of Campfire, people have grown to like the animals. When people see an elephant, they see money," explains Jack Nhiliziyo, Tsholotsho's district manager.

Hunting also pays for conservation. The National Parks and Wildlife Department, which gets 20% of hunting fees, uses the funds to pump water for elephants in the Hwange National Park and to pay for antipoaching patrols along the shores on Lake Kariba, a favorite raiding ground for Zambia-based poachers. Without hunting, concludes a recent report by the National Parks and Wildlife Department, "it is surely not possible for the government, which is battling with inflation, human poverty and escalating foreign debt, to meet all of these costs for all parks."

The Campfire program is not perfect—but the way to fix much of what is wrong with it is to allow *more* hunting. The villages decide how the money is spent by majority vote. The minority who lost crops are often outvoted by the many who want a concrete well or meeting hall with a metal roof. "If we continued the compensation [to victims]," declares Tsholotsho council Chairman Mthembo, "we will have no projects." More hunting revenue could spare these poor villages from such cruel choices.

Zimbabwe is using hunting to check the surging elephant population, enhance wildlife habitat and enable villagers and elephants to live in harmony. If Sen. Boxer saw Campfire at work, she might buy a hunting license.

> "By recognizing that natural environments must be maintained for successful economic development, rural populations are using ecotourism to generate income and spur habitat preservation."

Ecotourism Preserves Biodiversity

Abigail Rome

Abigail Rome argues in the following viewpoint that ecotourism preserves biodiversity because it provides local people with a lucrative alternative to destructive uses of natural resources and makes sustainable development possible. In Brazil, she maintains, ecotourism protects fish stocks and fishermen's livelihoods, preserves the remaining rain forest, and provides income for local people. Rome is a freelance writer and consultant in conservation and ecotourism based in Washington, D.C.

As you read, consider the following questions:
1. What threatens fish stocks in Brazil's heartland, according to Rome?
2. According to the author, what program does ASPAC's ecotourism fund?
3. In the author's opinion, what is the animal that most attracts tourists to eastern Brazil?

Reprinted from "Amazon Adventure," by Abigail Rome, *E/The Environmental Magazine*, March/April 1999, with permission from *E/The Environmental Magazine*, Subscription Dept.: PO Box 2047, Marion, OH 43306; ph. (815) 734-1242. Subscriptions are $20 per year.

Imagine a lone fisherman quietly and gracefully paddling his dugout canoe through the submerged grasses of an Amazonian lake. He is there today, following a centuries-old tradition of nourishing his family with the many species of fish which once proliferated in the world's largest river basin. A few years ago, however, his future was not so secure. In his island community of Silves, 180 miles east of Manaus in Brazil's heartland, fish stocks are threatened by population growth, improved fishing technologies and destruction of habitat. But a group of far-sighted residents have gotten involved to ensure that the fisherman's way of life does not disappear. For support, they've turned to an unlikely source: ecotourists wanting to experience life in the Amazon.

Ecotourism Preserves Biodiversity

Silves is one of a growing number of communities in Brazil embracing ecotourism and biodiversity conservation as a means to securing a healthy future. By recognizing that natural environments must be maintained for successful economic development, rural populations are using ecotourism to generate income and spur habitat preservation. Although conditions and motivations differ from place to place, local livelihoods and global biodiversity benefit, and progress is made towards the universal goal of sustainable development.

Local people formed the Silves Association for Environmental and Cultural Preservation (ASPAC, in Portuguese) to establish and manage fish reserves. By declaring specific lakes off-limits for fishing, they created natural hatcheries to repopulate nearby rivers, many of which are also regulated by the association. ASPAC's ecotourism program provides funding for ranger patrols, education of the fishing community and habitat restoration. At Aldeia dos Lagos, a simple lodge over-looking the open river and lake systems of the Urubu River, visitors can relax with comfortable accommodations, fresh fish, local fruit and vegetable specialties, and an array of ecotours. Trained guides take visitors out on the water in motorized canoes or hiking through the forest.

Far away in the Atlantic coastal forest, farmers are finding that ecotourism can generate more income than agriculture, while also conserving the precious five percent of this forest

Ecotourism Helps Preserve the Rain Forest

Economics drive much of the world's habitat and natural resource destruction. Attempting to provide for their families, local people have cleared rain forests to grow crops, raise cattle, or harvest timber. This predicament creates a pressing need to provide locals with alternative income sources which will deter deforestation and other habitat loss. Developing ecologically sustainable enterprises—businesses which rely upon, but do not destroy, natural resources—is one such alternative.

The Ecotourism Program believes that tourism offers promise as an ecologically sustainable enterprise and alternate to rain-forest destruction.

Conservation International, www.ecotour.org, 1999.

that remains. The key here is the golden lion tamarin, a highly endangered monkey found only in eastern Brazil. Tamarins are an attraction for tourists, who want to see these brilliant animals caressing their young and swinging playfully through forest canopies. They are also of interest to scientists and conservationists, who relocate groups of monkeys barely surviving in small isolated forest patches to larger remnant forests on public and private lands. Farmers who own and agree to protect large tracts of forests can receive these tamarins and then generate income by inviting paying visitors to see them.

Ecotourists Save Endangered Species

Luis Nelson, owner of Fazenda Bom Retiro, is an enterprising farmer and forest owner protecting tamarins and enticing tourists. He has built a lodge for 12 visitors, created a pond and arching waterfall which gives back-pounding massages, and planted gardens to attract hummingbirds, butterflies and other wildlife. Luis receives guests on his flower-filled dining patio, presenting them with a spectacular assortment of locally-grown fruits, vegetables and homemade Brazilian fare. He delights in guiding guests through his forest, showing off unique wild plants, including Brazil's only native banana—small and sweet, with large, tooth-breaking seeds. All the while, he is on the lookout for tamarins. Glimpses of gold swinging through the treetops are cherished by farmer and tourist alike. For Luis and his neighbors, money and environmental pride are the rewards. For the ecotourist, there is the exhilaration of seeing this brilliant creature free in the forest, knowing that one's presence supports the tamarin's continued existence.

Three hours from the capital city of Brasilia is another protected area where communities make their living from ecotourism. Chapada dos Veadeiros National Park is in the middle of one of the largest savanna-forest complexes in the world, the cerrado, containing a third of Brazil's plant and animal species. Residents of the nearby Sao Jorge village have demonstrated their commitment to making tourism a key element of their economic future by establishing the Chapada dos Veadeiros Tourist Guide Association. The organization offers courses and provides certification in environmental interpretation and guiding. Residents who once made their living as miners, exploiting quartz crystals, are now preserving the land, proudly showing off spectacular waterfalls and unique fauna and flora to visitors from every corner of the globe. The community has raised its standard of living through hotel management and tourist guiding, as well as production of jams and wild flowers for sale to tourists and for export. At the same time, the cerrado community is conserved and appreciated locally and globally.

> *"You won't get proper ecotourists to stay unless you set up shop in a virgin rain forest that is chock-a-block full of endangered species—precisely where you'll do the most damage."*

Ecotourism Does Not Preserve Biodiversity

Adam J. Freedman

In the following viewpoint, Adam J. Freedman maintains that ecotourism damages biodiversity because it encourages economic development in sensitive wilderness areas. Ecotourism is fueled by the guilt and hypocrisy of environmentalists, he contends, who want to enjoy consumer privileges that actually harm the environment. Freedman is an attorney practicing in New York.

As you read, consider the following questions:
1. According to Freedman, how much money does ecotourism generate annually?
2. What do scientists claim is special about Costa Rica, according to Freedman?
3. What has been blamed for the decline of the cheetah population in Kenya, according to the author?

Reprinted, with permission, from "EcoTopia," by Adam J. Freedman, *National Review*, December 11, 1995. Copyright ©1995 by National Review, Inc., www.nationalreview.com.

O n my first morning in Costa Rica, the world capital of "ecotourism," I awoke to find a maid diligently spraying insecticide just outside my window. Poor thing, she did not realize that a good ecotourist enjoys a healthy biodiversity in his hotel room.

She'll learn. Ecotourism, which began as a left-wing offshoot of the adventure travel business, is the fastest growing sector in the tourism industry, worth well over $200 billion a year. It is loosely described as tourism which has a "low impact" on the environment and which contributes to the local economy (and what kind of tourism doesn't?). Ecotourism has therefore grown to encompass everything out of doors, save blood sports. If you like a good walk in the woods, you may be an ecotourist too.

Liberal Guilt

The success of ecotourism is fueled by that endlessly renewable resource, liberal guilt; in this case caused by the fact that people occasionally need to take vacations even while the rain forest is dying. Smart hotel and tour operators have created packages that offer tourists a chance to "do something" about the environment while on vacation. In response, thousands of busybodies are marching south, like a parade of army ants, in search of a guilt-free holiday.

Fun-free too, by the look of things. The dismally purposive activities on offer include researching the habitats of blue whales, experimenting with herbal remedies for AIDS, and testing water samples in the Bahamas. Perhaps the greatest irony is that the liberal classes, who pioneered the idea of paying people not to work, are so thoroughly opposed to any form of unbridled leisure.

Third World governments, from Indonesia to Ecuador, are actively promoting ecotourism as a source of foreign exchange. Costa Rica, a country the size of West Virginia wedged between Nicaragua and Panama, is the undisputed leader of the field.

Costa Rica's eco-chic must be attributed in part to the Left's adoration of that country's politics. Army-less (thanks to the U.S. guarantee of its neutrality), democratic, and perennially incapable of hosting a decent coup, the country has been described as a slice of Scandinavia in Central America. Costa Rica also happens to be, as the scientists say, a "biological bridge" between North and South America, hosting a tremendous variety of wildlife. It is, in fact, a country of great physical beauty (if one may impose a value judgment).

Superficial Sensitivity

Monteverde is an obligatory stop for all ecotourists in Costa Rica, because it is in a "cloudforest," which is what you call a rain forest on a mountainside. Monteverde was founded by American Quakers who refused to subsidize the Pentagon with their tax dollars (but evidently had no objection to the tax-free benefits of the Monroe Doctrine). Their lasting legacies are a cheese factory and a strict left-wing party line.

Which is the first problem with ecotourism: wherever it holds sway, you can bet that a perfectly pleasant vacation will be spoiled by incessant liberal proselytizing. For example, during one tour of Monteverde the guide announced: "I am sure that you do not agree with the philosophy of a certain Mr. Reagan, who said 'seen one tree, seen 'em all.'" One tour participant delivered a heartfelt apology simply for being American.

Dead Cheetah Cubs

Cherise Miller [an ecotourist] was similarly put off by her trip into the Peruvian Amazon with [an] outfitter. "They advertised it as being an ecotourism facility with a world-record variety of birds . . . but on the first night they said, 'We're going to take you caiman hunting.'" A boat set out at dusk to search for the alligatorlike reptiles. A guide spotted a baby, jumped into the river and caught it. "Everyone in the boat passed along the baby caiman, taking pictures," says Miller.

Ecotourism can and does go awry anywhere. Megan Epler Wood of the Ecotourism Society says that timber around Nepal's Himalayan trails has been stripped to heat water for tea-sipping trekkers. Ruth Norris, a nature guide and ecotourism adviser, talks about cheetah-chasing ecosafaris in Kenya. "A mother cheetah was so panicked by all these tourists, she killed her cubs."

Caroline Arlen, *U.S. News & World Report*, May 29, 1995.

The ecotourist orthodoxy combines superficial sensitivity with a profound contempt toward the local population. All roads to prosperity, other than ecotourism, are suspect. The ecotourists particularly condemn Costa Rica's growing agricultural sector because crops and grazing lead to deforestation. However, ecotourist-driven land speculation has raised the price of pastureland to the point where grazing may cease to be a "problem." The country is now more dependent on the whims of left-wing trendsetters than on its banana exports.

Ecotourism Is Counterproductive

Of course, there is another, larger problem with ecotourism: it is counterproductive. It is, after all, a trend which encourages economic development of the wilderness. And not just any old wilderness. You won't get proper ecotourists to stay unless you set up shop in a virgin rain forest that is chock-a-block full of endangered species—precisely where you'll do the most damage.

For example, in Nepal, one village alone has had to cut down a hectare of virgin rhododendron forest each year in order to heat the meals and baths of eco-trekkers. This, in turn, causes soil erosion, landslides, and floods. Not long ago, a ship carrying 300 ecotourists ran aground off Antarctica. Because it was deemed too expensive to salvage, the ship was abandoned and has spilled 250,000 gallons of oil into an area where some 20,000 penguins nest. In Kenya, obliging guides take their jeeps off trail so that ecotourists can get a better look at the animals they're saving. The practice is now blamed for the decline of the cheetah population in at least one wildlife park.

Meanwhile, back in the rain forest, Costa Rica's Manuel Antonio Park is getting 1,000 tourists a day—who unwittingly turned the famous howler monkeys into garbage foragers. On top of this, Costa Rica has one of the fastest rates of deforestation in the world, ranking first in Latin America for percentage of deforested land.

The inescapable fact is that ecotourism, even when tastefully advertised on recycled paper, is intrusive. Naturally (so to speak), the ecotourists cannot appreciate that the wilderness—like the economy—is best left alone.

Periodical Bibliography

The following articles have been selected to supplement the diverse views presented in this chapter. Addresses are provided for periodicals not indexed in the *Readers' Guide to Periodical Literature*, the *Alternative Press Index*, the *Social Sciences Index*, or the *Index to Legal Periodicals and Books*.

Animal People	"Shipboard with the Sea Shepherds," September 1997. Available from PO Box 960, Clinton, WA 98236-0960.
Karl Hess Jr.	"Wild Success," *Reason*, October 1997.
Michelle E. Howard and Clifford E. Thies	"The Invisible Hand That Has, Time and Again, Saved the Whales," *St. Croix Review*, February 1995. Available from PO Box 244, Stillwater, MN 55082.
Steve Kemper	"The 'Sea Canary' Sings the Blues," *Smithsonian*, November 1999.
Richard Miniter	"Too Many Elephants," *Wall Street Journal*, July 17, 1997.
Cynthia Moss	"Elephants Slaughtered," *HSUS News*, Spring 1995. Available from the Humane Society, 2100 L St. NW, Washington, DC 20037.
James D. Nations and Michael Saxenian	"Guatemalan Reserve Is a Model Biosphere," *Forum for Applied Research and Public Policy*, Spring 1998. Available from PO Box 52146, Knoxville, TN 37950-2146.
Richard C. Paddock	"Outfoxing Limits on Whaling," *Los Angeles Times*, September 14, 1997. Available from Times Mirror Square, Los Angeles, CA 90053.
David Andrew Price	"Save the Whalers," *American Spectator*, Fall 1995.
Elaine Robbins	"Whale Watch," *E/The Environmental Magazine*, May/June 1997.
David Taylor	"Saving the Forest for the Trees: Alternative Products from Woodlands," *Environment*, January/February 1997.

For Further Discussion

Chapter 1

1. Edward J. Maruska cites statistics to support his contention that extinction is a serious problem. Robert W. Lee counters that argument by providing examples of rediscovered species once thought extinct. Are you more convinced by Maruska's evidence or Lee's? Explain your answer.

2. Alston Chase argues that extinction is not only a natural occurrence but often a beneficial one, yet George Wuerthner calls extinction "one of the gravest threats to native wildlife and plants." What evidence does each writer present to support his position and which argument do you find more convincing? Why?

3. Kelly Luker claims that the loss of biodiversity associated with modern breeding practices of domestic livestock threatens our food supply and is an "economic and social disaster in the making." Do you agree with her argument? Why or why not? Which do you feel is more important, protecting threatened livestock breeds or saving endangered wildlife like tigers and owls? Explain your answer.

Chapter 2

1. Jeff Jacoby supports his argument that the Endangered Species Act is ineffective by pointing out that species have been saved through governmental and private actions not governed by the regulation. However, Robert Kahn argues that those actions would never have taken place without the Endangered Species Act. In your opinion, would conservation efforts be made without the pressure that governmental regulation creates? Explain your answer.

2. John Terborgh and Michael Soule argue for the establishment of reserve networks even though one component of them—wildlife corridors—are as yet untested. Don Loucks questions the science behind reserve networks and claims that such megareserves would harm people without any guarantee of improved biodiversity. Do you think conservation plans of such magnitude should be attempted without proof that they will succeed? In your opinion, can science ever provide the kind of guarantees that Loucks demands? Explain your answer.

3. Julianne Couch and Tracey Rembert argue that breeding black-footed ferrets and reintroducing them into the wild has been successful because 349 specimens are being held in captivity

and 100 released in the wild. However, the Captive Animal Protection Society argues that 90 percent of the ferrets released will die. Does the omission of mortality rates in Couch's and Rembert's viewpoint affect the credibility of their argument? Do you accept the Captive Animal Protection Society's statistics without knowing their source? Overall, which viewpoint uses the most convincing evidence to support its argument? Explain your answer.

Chapter 3

1. Marlo Lewis maintains that an individual's right to own and manage private property without governmental restriction is the foundation of civil liberty. Douglas Chadwick, on the other hand, argues that sometimes individuals must sacrifice their individual rights in order to protect the rights of the citizenry as a whole. Does the loss of an endangered species like the northern spotted owl harm the common good? Explain. Whose viewpoint, Lewis's or Chadwick's, do you find most convincing and why?

2. Tom McDonnell argues that wolf reintroduction programs have increased ranchers' livestock losses and hurt them financially. Andre Carothers, on the other hand, maintains that livestock losses to ranchers are minimal and that ranchers have been reimbursed for any losses sustained. In your opinion, which author provides the most convincing evidence in support of his argument? Explain your answer.

3. The organization, Save Our Wild Salmon, argues that corporations will not support plans to save salmon unless forced to do so by the Endangered Species Act. Clay Landry argues that forcing corporations and farmers to save salmon by listing them on the endangered species list would actually damage efforts to save them. Do you agree with Landry that landowners need financial incentives in order to preserve endangered species? Or do you agree with Save Our Wild Salmon that only the force of governmental regulation will guarantee conservation? What are the pros and cons of each author's argument?

Chapter 4

1. Halldór Ásgrímsson argues that sustainable whaling of species that are not endangered is vital to the economies of many nations like Iceland and should be internationally supported. The World Wildlife Fund calls for a ban on all commercial whaling. In your opinion, which author supports his argument more effectively? Explain. Do you think nations need to protect all whales by supporting a ban on all commercial whaling or

should some commercial whaling of non-endangered species be allowed for countries who can prove they have economic need? Explain your answer.

2. Richard Miniter contends that hunting makes elephants an economic asset which encourages local people to protect them. On the other hand, Matthew Scully maintains that hunting can never protect elephants because it only serves the short-term interests of people motivated by personal gain and leads to overexploitation. Do you think that self-interest—wanting to profit from elephant hunting, for example—can ever be channeled to support collective goals like saving elephants? If so, how? Or do you believe that people must be required by law to support goals whose benefits may not be felt by them directly? Explain your answer.

3. Abigail Rome argues that ecotourism provides local people with alternative ways to make money without destroying the rain forests. However, Adam J. Freeman maintains that ecotourism merely provides expensive entertainment to guilt-ridden environmentalists who actually harm the environment on their trips. In your opinion, do you think vacationing in sensitive areas like the rain forest is the best way to save endangered species and protect habitats? Explain your answer.

4. International conservation efforts like whaling and hunting bans are often initiated by countries such as the United States that have limited knowledge or understanding of the consequences felt by the affected countries once the ban is in place. Do you agree that the United States is right to get involved in how other countries manage their natural resources? Why or why not?

Organizations to Contact

The editors have compiled the following list of organizations concerned with the issues debated in this book. The descriptions are derived from materials provided by the organizations. All have publications or information available for interested readers. The list was compiled on the date of publication of the present volume; the information provided here may change. Be aware that many organizations take several weeks or longer to respond to inquiries, so allow as much time as possible.

American Forest and Paper Association (AFPA)
1111 19th St. NW, Suite 800, Washington, DC 20036
(202) 463-2700 • fax: (202) 463-2471
e-mail: info@afandpa.org • website: www.afandpa.org
AFPA is a national trade association of the forest, pulp, paper, paperboard, and wood products industry. The association publishes materials on timber supply and forest management as well as the *International Trade Report*, a monthly newsletter that features articles on current issues affecting forest products, industry, and international trade.

American Livestock Breeds Conservancy (ALBC)
PO Box 477, Pittsboro, NC 27312
(919) 542-5704 • fax: (919) 545-0022
e-mail: albc@albc-usa.org • website: www.albc-usa.org
ALBC works to prevent the extinction of rare breeds of American livestock. The conservancy believes that conservation is necessary to protect the genetic range and survival ability of these species. ALBC provides general information about the importance of saving rare breeds as well as specific guidelines for individuals interested in raising rare breeds.

American Zoo and Aquarium Association (AZA)
8403 Colesville Rd., Suite 710, Silver Spring, MD 20910
(301) 562-0777 • fax: (301) 562-0888
website: www.aza.org
AZA represents over 160 zoos and aquariums in North America. The association provides information on captive breeding of endangered species, conservation education, natural history, and wildlife legislation. AZA publications include the *Species Survival Plans* and the *Annual Report on Conservation and Science*.

Atlantic Salmon Federation (ASF)
PO Box 807, Calais, ME 04619-0807
(506) 529-1033 • fax: (506) 529-4438
e-mail: asf@nbnet.nb.ca • website: www.asf.ca

ASF is an international nonprofit organization that promotes the conservation and wise management of the wild Atlantic salmon and its environment. It publishes the *Atlantic Salmon Journal*, the world's oldest publication for the conservation-minded salmon angler.

Canadian Forestry Association (CFA)
185 Somerset St. W, Suite 203, Ottawa, ON K2P 0J2 Canada
(613) 232-1815 • fax: (613) 232-4210
website: www.canadian-forests.com

CFA works for improved forest management that would satisfy the economic, social, and environmental demands on Canadian forests. The association explores conflicting perspectives on forestry-related topics in its biannual *Forest Forum*.

Captive Animal Protection Society (CAPS)
PO Box 43, Dudley DY3 2YP, England
Phone/fax: 01384-456682
e-mail: diane@caps-uk.dircon.co.uk
website: www.caps-uk.dircon.co.uk

CAPS was established in 1957 and is recognized today as one of the United Kingdom's leading campaigning organizations on behalf of animals in circuses, zoos, and the entertainment industry. CAPS is opposed to the use of performing animals in circuses.

Conservation International (CI)
2501 M St. NW, Suite 200, Washington, DC 20037
(202) 429-5660 • fax (202) 887-0193
e-mail: info@conservation.org
website: www.conservation.org

CI believes that the earth's natural heritage must be maintained if future generations are to thrive spiritually, culturally, and economically. CI's mission is to conserve the earth's living natural heritage, our global biodiversity, and to demonstrate that human societies are able to live harmoniously with nature.

Defenders of Wildlife
1101 14th St. NW, Suite 1400, Washington, DC 20005
(202) 682-9400
e-mail: info@defenders.org • website: www.defenders.org

Defenders of Wildlife is dedicated to the protection of all native wild animals and plants in their natural communities. The organization focuses on the accelerating rate of extinction of species and the associated loss of biodiversity, and habitat alteration and destruction. The organization publishes *Defenders* magazine.

Endangered Species Coalition (ESC)

1101 14th St. NW, Suite 1200, Washington, DC 20005
(202) 682-9400 • fax: (202) 682-1331
e-mail: esc@stopextinction.org
website: www.stopextinction.org

The coalition is composed of conservation, professional, and animal welfare groups that work to extend the Endangered Species Act and to ensure its enforcement. ESC encourages public activism through grassroots organizations, direct lobbying, and letter-writing and telephone campaigns. Its publications include the book *The Endangered Species Act: A Commitment Worth Keeping* and articles, fact sheets, position papers, and bill summaries regarding the Endangered Species Act.

Foundation for Research on Economics and the Environment (FREE)

945 Technology Blvd., Suite 101F, Bozeman, MT 59718
(406) 585-1776 • fax: (406) 585-3000
website: www.free-eco.org

FREE is a research and education foundation committed to freedom, environmental quality, and economic progress. The foundation works to reform environmental policy by using the principles of private property rights, the free market, and the rule of law. FREE publishes the quarterly newsletter *FREE Perspective on Economics and the Environment* and produces a biweekly syndicated op-ed column.

International Society of Tropical Foresters (ISTF)

5400 Grosvenor Ln., Bethesda, MD 20814
(301) 897-8720 • fax: (301) 897-3690
e-mail: istf@igc.apc.org

ISTF is a nonprofit international organization that strives to develop and promote ecologically sound methods of managing and harvesting tropical forests. The society provides information and technical knowledge about the effect of deforestation on agriculture, forestry, and industry. It publishes the quarterly newsletter *ISTF News*.

National Wildlife Federation (NWF)
8925 Leesburg Pike, Vienna, VA 22184
(703) 790-4000
website: www.nwf.org

The federation encourages the intelligent management of our natural resources and promotes the appreciation of such resources. It operates Ranger Rick's Wildlife Camp and sponsors National Wildlife Week. It also has a large library of conservation-related publications, which include *Ranger Rick's Nature Magazine* and *National Wildlife Magazine*.

North American Wolf Association (NAWA)
23214 Tree Bright St., Spring, TX 77373
(281) 821-4884
website: www.nawa.org

NAWA is a nonprofit organization dedicated to wolf recovery, reintroduction, rescue, and preservation.

PERC
502 S. 19th Ave., Bozeman, MT 59718
(406) 587-9591 • fax: (406) 586-7555
e-mail: perc@perc.org • website: www.perc.org

PERC is a research center that provides solutions to environmental problems based on free market principles and the importance of property rights. PERC publications include the quarterly newsletter *PERC Report* and papers in the *PERC Policy Series* dealing with environmental issues.

Rainforest Action Network (RAN)
221 Pine St., Suite 500, San Francisco, CA 94104
(415) 398-4404 • fax: (415) 398-2732
e-mail: rainforest@ran.org • website: www.ran.org

RAN works to preserve the world's rain forests and protect the rights of native forest-dwelling peoples. The network sponsors letter-writing campaigns, boycotts, and demonstrations in response to environmental concerns. It publishes miscellaneous fact sheets, the monthly *Action Alert Bulletin*, and the quarterly *World Rainforest Report*.

U.S. Fish and Wildlife Service
Office of Public Affairs, 1849 C St. NW, Washington, DC 20240
(202) 208-5634
website: www.fws.gov

The U.S. Fish and Wildlife Service is a network of regional offices, national wildlife refuges, research and development centers, national fish hatcheries, and wildlife law enforcement agencies. The service's primary goal is to conserve, protect, and enhance fish and wildlife and their habitats. It publishes an endangered species list as well as facts sheets, pamphlets, and information on the Endangered Species Act.

World Wildlife Fund (WWF)
1250 24th St. NW, PO Box 97180, Washington, DC 20077-7180
(800) 225-5993
website: www.worldwildlife.org

WWF works to save endangered species, to conduct wildlife research, and to improve the natural environment. It publishes an endangered species list, the bimonthly newsletter *Focus*, and a variety of books on the environment.

Bibliography of Books

Diane Ackerman — *The Rarest of the Rare: Vanishing Animals, Timeless Worlds.* New York: Random House, 1995.

Terry L. Anderson and Donald R. Leal — *Enviro-Capitalists: Doing Good While Doing Well.* Lanham, MD: Rowman and Littlefield, 1997.

Rodney Barker — *And the Waters Turned to Blood: The Ultimate Biological Threat.* New York: Simon & Schuster, 1997.

Yvonne Baskin — *The Work of Nature: How the Diversity of Life Sustains Us.* Washington, DC: Island Press, 1997.

Walton Beacham and Kirk H. Beetz, eds. — *Beacham's Guide to International Endangered Species.* Osprey, FL: Beacham Publishing, 1998.

Katrina Brandon — *Ecotourism and Conservation: A Review of Key Issues.* Washington, DC: World Bank, 1996.

Chris Bright — *Life Out of Bounds: Bioinvasion in a Borderless World.* New York: Norton, 1998.

J. Baird Callicott and Michael P. Nelson, eds. — *The Great New Wilderness Debate.* Athens: University of Georgia Press, 1998.

Joseph Cone — *A Common Fate: Endangered Salmon and the People of the Northwest.* New York: Holt, 1995.

James DeLong — *Property Matters: How Property Rights Are Under Assault—And Why You Should Care.* New York: Free Press, 1997.

Paul R. Ehrlich and Anne H. Ehrlich — *Betrayal of Science and Reason: How Anti-Environmental Rhetoric Threatens Our Future.* Washington, DC: Island Press, 1996.

Gary Ferguson — *The Yellowstone Wolves: The First Year.* Helena, MT: Falcon Press, 1996.

Hank Fischer — *Wolf Wars: The Remarkable Inside Story of the Restoration of Wolves to Yellowstone.* Helena, MT: Falcon Press, 1995.

Lesley France, ed. — *The Earthscan Reader in Sustainable Tourism.* London: Earthscan Publications, 1997.

Donald Goddard, ed. — *Saving Wildlife: A Century of Conservation.* New York: Abrams/Wildlife Conservation Society, 1995.

Martha Honey — *Ecotourism and Sustainable Development: Who Owns Paradise?* Washington, DC: Island Press, 1999.

Kay A. Kenyon — *Reintroduction of Captive Animals into Their Native Habitat.* Washington, DC: Smithsonian Institution, 1995.

Thomas Lambert

The Endangered Species Act: A Train Wreck Ahead. St. Louis, MO: Center for the Study of American Business, 1995.

Richard E. Leakey and Roger Lewin

The Sixth Extinction: Patterns of Life and the Future of Humankind. New York: Doubleday, 1995.

Charles C. Mann and Mark L. Plummer

Noah's Choice: The Future of Endangered Species. New York: Knopf, 1995.

William McCloskey

Their Father's Work: Casting Nets with the World's Fishermen. New York: McGraw-Hill, 1998.

Deborah McLaren

Rethinking Tourism and Ecotravel: The Paving of Paradise and What You Can Do To Stop It. West Hartford, CT: Kumarian Press, 1998.

Thomas McNamee

The Return of the Wolf to Yellowstone. New York: Holt, 1998.

Bryan G. Norton, ed.

Ethics on the Ark: Zoos, Animal Welfare, and Wildlife Conservation. Washington, DC: Smithsonian Institution, 1995.

Michael Jay Polonsky and Alma T. Mintu-Wimsatt, eds.

Environmental Marketing: Strategies, Practice, Theory and Research. Binghamton, NY: Haworth Press, 1995.

David Quammen

The Song of the Dodo: Island Biogeography in an Age of Extinctions. London: Hutchinson, 1996.

Clifford J. Sherry

Endangered Species: A Reference Handbook. Santa Barbara, CA: ABC-CLIO, 1998.

Jason F. Shogren and William Ruckelshaus

Private Property and the Endangered Species Act: Saving Habitats, Protecting Homes. Austin: University of Texas Press, 1999.

Bruce A. Stein and Stephanie R. Flack

America's Least Wanted: Alien Species Invasions of U.S. Ecosystems. Arlington, VA: Nature Conservancy, 1996.

Dugald Stermer

Vanishing Flora: Endangered Plants Around the World. New York: H.N. Abrams, 1995.

Peter J. Stoett

The International Politics of Whaling. Vancouver: University of British Columbia Press, 1997.

John R. Twiss and Randall R. Reeves, eds.

Conservation and Management of Marine Mammals. Washington, DC: Smithsonian Institution, 1999.

Ray Vaughan

Endangered Species Act Handbook. Rockville, MD: Government Institutes, 1994.

Bruce Yandle

Land Rights: The 1990's Property Rights Rebellion. Lanham, MD: Rowman and Littlefield, 1995.

Index